P9-CFN-384

The EVERYTHING KIDS' Cookbook

2ND EDITION

From mac 'n cheese to double chocolate chip cookies—
90 recipes to have some finger-lickin' fun

Sandra K. Nissenberg, M.S., R.D.

Aadamsmedia
Avon, Massachusetts

DISCLAIMER

NOTE: All activities in this book should be performed with adult supervision. Likewise, common sense and care are essential to the conduct of any and all activities, whether described in this book or otherwise. Neither the author nor the publisher assumes any responsibility for any injuries or damages arising from any activities.

PUBLISHER Karen Cooper

DIRECTOR OF ACQUISITIONS AND INNOVATION Paula Munier

MANAGING EDITOR, EVERYTHING SERIES Lisa Laing

COPY CHIEF Casey Ebert

ACQUISITIONS EDITOR Kerry Smith and Katie McDonough

DEVELOPMENT EDITOR Elizabeth Kassab

EDITORIAL ASSISTANT Hillary Thompson

Copyright © 2008 by F+W Media, Inc.
All rights reserved.
This book, or parts thereof, may not be reproduced in any form without permission from the publisher; exceptions are made for brief excerpts used in published reviews and photocopies made for classroom use.

An Everything® Series Book.
Everything® and everything.com® are registered trademarks of F+W Media, Inc.

Published by Adams Media, a division of F+W Media, Inc.
57 Littlefield Street, Avon, MA 02322. U.S.A.
www.adamsmedia.com

ISBN-10: 1-59869-592-4
ISBN-13: 978-1-59869-592-2

Printed by RR Donnelley, Owensville, MO, USA.

20 19 18 17 16 15 14 13

December 2015

This publication is designed to provide accurate and authoritative information with regard to the subject matter covered. It is sold with the understanding that the publisher is not engaged in rendering legal, accounting, or other professional advice. If legal advice or other expert assistance is required, the services of a competent professional person should be sought.
—From a *Declaration of Principles* jointly adopted by a Committee of the American Bar Association and a Committee of Publishers and Associations

Many of the designations used by manufacturers and sellers to distinguish their products are claimed as trademarks. When those designations appear in this book and Adams Media was aware of a trademark claim, the designations have been printed with initial capital letters.

Cover illustrations by Dana Regan.
Interior illustrations by Kurt Dolber.
Puzzles by Beth L. Blair.

This book is available at quantity discounts for bulk purchases.
For information, please call 1-800-289-0963.

Visit the entire Everything® series at *www.everything.com*

Contents

Introduction

Kids love to have fun, get messy, experiment, and be creative. Since cooking is all about those things, it's no wonder that kids love to cook.

When I first started writing kid's cookbooks more than fifteen years ago, my children were young. They enjoyed everything about being in the kitchen. They played with my pots and pans, my wooden spoons, and even my plastic containers. Whenever they asked to help, I found them something to do, whether it was washing and tearing lettuce for a salad, stirring up a batter, setting the table, or sampling a recipe. Now that they are teenagers, they have a better understanding of the ins and outs of meal planning, food preparation, and, of course, nutrition. As they move forward in their lives, they will have a strong foundation for being independent adults and teaching their future families good skills as well.

The first edition of *The Everything® Kids' Cookbook* was published in 2002, to encourage parents and kids to have fun in the kitchen. Since that time, we have seen a strong interest in kids' nutrition and the need to start teaching early so kids will enjoy happy, healthy lives as they get older. With the surge of childhood obesity in our society, now it is even more important to teach our kids about nutrition and how to manage their food intake. If we can get children interested in valuing their bodies and their food intake, making the right food choices, and managing their portion sizes, they will be off to the best start life has to offer.

With *The Everything® Kids' Cookbook, 2nd Edition*, we have kept much of the valued information found in the first edition while updating resources and nutrition information that may have changed in recent years. We have also added some new recipes, but kept many of your old favorites. The book continues to incorporate fun, too. You'll still find games, puzzles, and fun food trivia that will make your day a little brighter.

Kids (and adults) will continue to enjoy everything that *The Everything® Kids' Cookbook, 2nd Edition* has to offer. And remember, the most important lesson of all is to build strong memories with your families that will last a lifetime.

Happy, healthy eating to you and your family.

Sandy K. Nissenberg

While cooking, children must be supervised by a responsible adult at all times.

Chapter 1
Let's Get Cooking

Tasty Tuna Melt

Tuna melts make a great lunch, and they're also great to share as an afternoon snack. For a fun change, bake a potato in the microwave, top it with tuna and cheese, and bake it. You will have a Tuna Melt Potato!

▶ **DIFFICULTY: MEDIUM** ◀ - - -

Makes 4 tuna melt sandwich halves

2 English muffins or bagels, split in half
1 6-ounce can chunk tuna, canned in water, drained
2 tablespoons mayonnaise
¼ cup shredded or sliced cheese: Cheddar, mozzarella, or American

1. Preheat the oven to 350°F.
2. Place English muffin or bagel halves onto a cookie sheet or a sheet of aluminum foil.
3. Use the can opener to open the tuna, then carefully drain the water.
4. In a small bowl, combine the drained tuna with the mayonnaise. Mix well.
5. Top each English muffin or bagel half with tuna, then with the cheese.
6. Bake 5–8 minutes, or until the cheese is melted.

The best things about cooking are that you can be creative, experiment, and share what you make. Like any activity that involves experiments, there are tools, terms, and things to know so that the only surprise in your kitchen is how easy cooking can be.

The next few sections aren't as exciting as making Cereal Necklaces (Page 124) or Chocolate-Peanut Butter Pudding (Page 120), but they are pretty important. Otherwise, how will you know whether to bake or boil? Slice or mash?

Read this chapter with your parents or the adult who will be helping you in the kitchen. The recipes are written for you, but it's important for all the cooks to know what's going on.

Reading Recipes

Recipes are a set of instructions for making a particular food. It is important to read the recipe carefully so you understand how to make the food and what ingredients you will need to make it. A typical recipe could include the following:

★ Level of difficulty
★ Tools of the trade
★ Quantity (or number of servings) that the recipe makes
★ An ingredient list
★ Oven temperature (if necessary)
★ Easy-to-understand instructions
★ Baking or cooking times

Important Safety Tips and Kitchen Rules:

Safety should be your number-one priority when working and cooking in the kitchen. Hot food or pans, boiling water, and sharp knives can all be dangerous if you don't know how to handle them properly. Always check with an adult or parent before working in the kitchen, and be sure to review these handy safety tips and kitchen rules before starting:

- **Be sure to wash your hands with soap and water before touching food.** It is also important to wash your hands right after you handle raw meat, chicken, or fish before you start touching other things.
- **Tie back long hair and pull up long sleeves.** First, you want to keep them out of your food. Second, for safety reasons you need to keep long or loose items away from things like blenders or the flame on your stove.
- **Read the entire recipe before you begin.** Find out what ingredients and utensils you will need. You'll also want to know how long a recipe takes to prepare and how many people it will feed.
- **Make a shopping list of things you need.** Include items you will need to keep the kitchen well stocked (such as sugar, eggs, or milk). Some items you may have to buy, but you may have others in your house already.
- **Start with a clean cooking area.** Otherwise, dirty dishes will be in your way, dirty counters will ruin your food, and other things on the counter or table (like mail) may get stained or splashed while you cook.
- **Don't overfill pots and pans.** If they overflow while you are cooking, you will definitely end up with a mess, and you might get splattered or splashed with hot liquids.

- **Know how to use the various appliances and utensils you will need.** If you need to, ask an adult to teach or remind you, especially if you are using anything with hot oil (like a wok) or sharp moving parts (like a food processor).
- **Be careful with knives.** Learn how to hold them, wash them, and store them properly.
- **Put ingredients away when you have finished with them.** Also, be sure to wipe down, unplug, and turn off all appliances when you're done.
- **Wipe counters clean while working.** Put dirty dishes in the sink to keep them away from the clean ones.
- **Keep electric appliances away from water or the sink.** Also, try to keep the cords up on the counter so you don't trip or step on them by accident.
- **Always use potholders or oven mitts to touch hot pans and dishes.** You may not realize how hot something is until you've touched it or picked it up, so it's always better to start out with your hands protected.
- **Know where to find things and where to put them away.** By keeping everything in its place, you will have a clean cooking area and you won't lose things.
- **Do only one job at a time.** Cooking requires planning and concentration—it's a lot like juggling! As you practice, you can do more and more, but in the beginning, just focus on one thing.
- **Get help.** Adults should supervise all your food preparation and cooking activities. It's important for you to learn how to work in a kitchen—and enjoy it!—but it's also important that you remember safety. Make sure an adult knows exactly what you are doing and will be able to give help if you need it.

The recipes in this book list the tools in advance so you know if you have everything you will need. The information about difficulty is pretty helpful for you, too. Some recipes can go from HARD to EASY just by having an adult do the cutting with sharp knives—it's that simple!

Tools of the Trade

Proper tools and utensils are a must for preparing food. Let's take a look at some of the most common cooking utensils and equipment you can find in the kitchen . . .

 Baking pan—a square or rectangular pan (glass or metal) used for baking and cooking food in the oven

Blender—an electric appliance used for blending liquids and grinding food

Can opener—a tool, either manual or electric, designed to open cans

Casserole dish—a glass dish, usually a 1-quart or 2-quart size, used to make casseroles or baked goods in the oven

 Colander—a metal (or sometimes plastic) bowl with holes in it used to drain water or liquid from foods (such as pasta or vegetables)

 Cookie sheet—a flat metal sheet used for baking cookies or other nonrunny items

 Cutting board—a board made from wood or hard plastic used when cutting or chopping ingredients

 Electric mixer—an electric appliance used for mixing ingredients (like cake batter) together

 Glass measuring cup—a glass cup, used to measure liquids, with various measurements printed along the side

 Ice cream scoop—a plastic or metal tool, shaped like a giant spoon, used to scoop ice cream from a carton

 Kitchen shears—scissors for the kitchen that can be used to cut herbs and other foods

 Measuring cups—plastic or metal cups in different sizes, used to measure dry ingredients, like sugar or flour

 Microwave oven—a small oven that cooks or reheats food very quickly by cooking with electromagnetic waves (microwaves)

 Mixing bowls—bowls (in various sizes) in which you mix ingredients together

 Muffin tins—metal or glass pans with small, round cups used for baking muffins and cupcakes

 Oven—a kitchen appliance for baking or broiling food

 Oven mitts/potholders—mittens or pads used to hold hot pots, pans, baking sheets, and plates

Parfait glass—a special glass used to serve parfaits; it usually has a wide mouth and a narrower bottom

 Pastry brush—a small brush used to spread melted butter, margarine, or sauces over food

 Pizza cutter—a tool with a rolling cutter used to easily cut pizzas, doughs, or breads

 Plate—a flat dish used to serve food

 Potato masher—a tool used to mash cooked potatoes, or anything soft, to make them smooth

 Rolling pin—a wooden or plastic roller used to flatten an item such as dough for a piecrust

 Saucepan—a pot with a projecting handle used for stovetop cooking

 Serving spoon—a large spoon used to scoop out large portions of food

 Skillet—a pan used for frying, stir-frying, and sautéing food in hot fat or oil

 Spatula—a plastic utensil used to fold foods together or scrape down batter from mixing bowls. You can use a flat metal utensil to lift, turn, and flip foods like eggs, cookies, and hamburgers.

 Stove—a kitchen appliance with gas or electric burners used for cooking food (also called a range or cooktop)

 Toaster Oven—a small oven that sits on the kitchen counter used to toast, bake, or even broil a small amount of food

 Vegetable peeler—sometimes called a potato or carrot peeler, used to peel the skin off of fruit or vegetables

 Whisk—a utensil used for mixing and stirring liquid ingredients, like eggs and milk, together

Wooden spoon—a big spoon made out of wood that is used for mixing and stirring just about any kind of food

Things to Know Before You Begin

It can sometimes be confusing to understand all the words used to describe different ways to prepare and cook foods in a recipe. Here is a reference guide to help.

Bake—to cook something inside the oven

Batter—a mixture made from ingredients like sugar, eggs, flour, and water that is used to make cakes, cookies, and pancakes

Beat—to mix hard and thoroughly with a spoon, fork, whisk, or electric mixer

Blend—to mix foods together until smooth

Boil—to cook in a liquid until bubbles appear or until a liquid reaches its boiling point (water boils at 212°F/100°C). *Note: Water cannot get hotter than its boiling point, it can only make steam faster.*

Broil—to put food under the broiler part of the oven, where the heat source is on top of the food

Brown—to cook at low to medium heat until food turns brown

Chill—to refrigerate food until it is cold

Chop—to cut food into small pieces with a knife, blender, or food processor

Cool—to let the food sit at room temperature until it is no longer hot

Cream—to mix ingredients like sugar, butter, and eggs together until they are smooth and creamy

Dice—to chop food into small, square (like dice), even-sized pieces

Drain—to pour off a liquid in which the food has been cooked or stored

Drizzle—to sprinkle drops of liquid, like chocolate syrup or an icing, lightly over the top of something, like cookies or a cake

Fold—to gently combine ingredients together from top to bottom until they are just mixed together

Grate—to shred food into tiny pieces with a shredder, grater, blender, or food processor

FIGURE 1-1: *Common cooking methods*

Bake   Boil   Simmer   Stir-fry

Crazy Cookbooks

Use the Letter-Number Key to fill in the blanks!

Key	
1 = A	5 = U
2 = E	6 = V
3 = I	7 = W
4 = O	8 = Y

1000 P _ ST _ D _ SH _ S, B _ M _ CK _ . R _ N _ _
‾1 ‾1 ‾3 ‾2 ‾8 ‾1 ‾1 ‾4 ‾2 ‾8

Q _ _ CK C _ _ K _ NG, B _ M _ KE R _ _ _ _ _
‾5 ‾3 ‾4 ‾4 ‾3 ‾8 ‾3 ‾2 ‾4 ‾2 ‾7 ‾1 ‾6 ‾2

_ MM _ _ _ G _ T BL _ S, B _ BR _ CK _ 'L _ GH
‾8 ‾5 ‾8 ‾6 ‾2 ‾2 ‾1 ‾2 ‾8 ‾4 ‾4 ‾2 ‾3

M _ X C _ N M _ LS, B _ _ UNT CH _ L _ D _
‾2 ‾3 ‾1 ‾2 ‾1 ‾8 ‾1 ‾3 ‾1 ‾1

L _ S _ _ GHT!, B _ C _ L _ . R _ Z _
‾4 ‾2 ‾7 ‾2 ‾3 ‾8 ‾1 ‾4 ‾2 ‾2 ‾2

Grease—to rub a baking pan or a dish with butter, margarine, or oil so food cooked on it won't stick (canned cooking spray will work, too)

Knead—to fold, press, and turn dough to make it the right consistency

Mash—to crush food into a soft mixture, like mashing potatoes

Mince—to cut food into very small pieces

Mix—to stir two or more ingredients together until they are evenly combined

Preheat—to turn the oven on to the desired temperature and let it heat up before putting the food in the oven

Purée—to mix in a blender or food processor until food is smooth and has the consistency of applesauce or a milkshake

Sauté—to cook food on the stovetop in a skillet with a little liquid or oil

Simmer—to cook over low heat until the food almost boils

Slice—to cut food into even-sized pieces

Steam—to put food over a pan of boiling water so the steam can cook it

Stir—to continuously mix food with a spoon

Stir-fry—to cook food on the stovetop in a very hot pan while stirring constantly

Toast—to brown the surface of a food by heating

Whip—to beat rapidly with a whisk, electric mixer, or eggbeater

Yummy!

Each of the clues suggests a word. Write the word on the dotted lines, then fill each letter into the grid. Work back and forth between the clues and the grid until you get the silly answer to the riddle.

A. Lettuce tossed with dressing

$\overline{}$ $\overline{}$ $\overline{}$ $\overline{}$ $\overline{}$
1 25 17 18 22

B. Melted rock from a volcano

$\overline{}$ $\overline{}$ $\overline{}$ $\overline{}$
26 16 12 14

C. Sound that bounces back

$\overline{}$ $\overline{}$ $\overline{}$ $\overline{}$
13 5 10 2

D. Back edge of the foot

$\overline{}$ $\overline{}$ $\overline{}$ $\overline{}$
3 24 21 8

E. An adult boy

$\overline{}$ $\overline{}$ $\overline{}$
23 11 19

F. A baby bear

$\overline{}$ $\overline{}$ $\overline{}$
20 7 15

G. A female deer

$\overline{}$ $\overline{}$ $\overline{}$
9 6 4

Why did the circus lion eat the tightrope walker?

1A	2C			3D	4G		
5C	6G	7F	8D	9G			
10C	11E	12B	13C		14B		
15F	16B	17A	18A	19E	20F	21D	22A
	23E	24D	25A	26B		!	

8

Measuring Ingredients

To make a recipe properly, it is necessary to measure ingredients accurately. Your cooking tools should include measuring spoons and a set of measuring cups for both liquid and dry ingredients.

Glass measuring cups are used to measure liquids like milk and water. These cups are marked with different measurements (¼ cup, ⅓ cup, ½ cup, ⅔ cup, ¾ cup, and 1 cup) so you can see how high to fill them.

Stacked measuring cups for dry ingredients come in specific sizes. The sets are usually made from either plastic or metal, and there are separate cups for each measurement. You usually use these cups for dry ingredients, like flour and sugar.

Measuring spoons measure small amounts of either liquid or dry ingredients.

Make sure to fill the cup or spoon evenly to the top. Level off dry ingredients using a blunt knife or spatula. Soft ingredients, like brown sugar, peanut butter, or shortening, get packed in, as shown in Figure 1-2.

FIGURE 1-2: **Measuring Methods**
Some ingredients are measured differently from others. These diagrams will help you.

Measuring Brown Sugar

Measuring Soft Ingredients

Measuring Liquid

Measuring Dry Ingredients

Measuring Butter

Using Measuring Spoon

Measuring Spoon Math

Margarita is baking a cake.
The recipe calls for: 2 cups flour
1 and ½ cups sugar
¼ cup cocoa powder

Margarita only has a tablespoon
with which to measure!
How many tablespoons (Tbsp.)
will she need of each ingredient?

Flour = _____ Tbsp.

Sugar = _____ Tbsp.

Cocoa = _____ Tbsp.

HINT: 16 Tbsp. = 1 cup

Common Cooking Abbreviations and Equivalent Measures

Most recipes use abbreviations for the measurements of your ingredients. Here is a quick guide to let you know what standard abbreviations mean:

TABLE 1-1 COMMON ABBREVIATIONS		
ABBREVIATION	=	MEASUREMENT
t. or tsp.	=	teaspoon
T. or Tbsp.	=	tablespoon
c.	=	cup
pt.	=	pint
qt.	=	quart
oz.	=	ounce
lb.	=	pound
pkg.	=	package

It is also helpful to know what different measurements equal. This quick reference will give you the basics:

TABLE 1-2		
RECIPE MEASUREMENT	=	WHAT IT EQUALS (EQUIVALENT)
a pinch/dash	=	less than ⅛ teaspoon
3 teaspoons	=	1 tablespoon
¼ cup	=	4 tablespoons
⅓ cup	=	5 tablespoons + 1 teaspoon
½ cup	=	8 tablespoons
⅔ cup	=	10 tablespoons + 2 teaspoons
½ pint	=	1 cup
1 cup (dry ingredients)	=	16 tablespoons
1 cup (liquid)	=	8 ounces
2 cups (liquid)	=	1 pint or ½ quart
4 cups (liquid)	=	1 quart
4 quarts (liquid)	=	1 gallon
8 ounces	=	½ pound
16 ounces	=	2 pints or ½ quart liquid
16 ounces	=	1 pound
32 ounces	=	1 quart
64 ounces	=	½ gallon
1 liter	=	1.06 quarts
1 quart	=	.95 liter

Nutrition to Know

Have you ever wondered why we eat? Or what we eat? We eat to keep nourished, to stay alive. Just like a car needs gasoline, people need fuel, and food is the fuel that keeps us moving. Without it, we could not survive.

Nutrients

Every food we eat has substances in it called nutrients. When we talk about nutrition, we are talking about these nutrients, all the substances that are in our food. There are more than fifty different nutrients—some you have probably heard of, like protein, fat, carbohydrates, vitamins, minerals, and even water. All these nutrients work together in our bodies to help us grow, give us energy, and help us stay healthy.

The Food Pyramid

To help people understand the importance of eating foods for good nutrition without having to study all the nutrients, the United States Department of Agriculture, or USDA, has developed a food pyramid. Called MyPyramid, it shows how much of each type of food people should eat each day. Your individual MyPyramid changes as you get older because you need different amounts and types of food as you grow. (You can find more information at *www.mypyramid.gov*.)

When you look at MyPyramid for Kids, you will notice all the colors of the rainbow moving up and down the pyramid. Each of these colors represents a specific food group, starting with the grain group on the far left all

the way across to the meat and beans group on the far right. In addition to sharing information about all the foods you need to eat, MyPyramid also encourages physical fitness. Learning about the importance of eating right and exercising will help you lead a healthy life.

Here are a few tips to help you understand the food groups and keep you moving down the right path toward good nutrition and exercise.

★ **Grains**—Make half of your grains whole; look for 100% whole-grain products like breads, cereals, pastas, rice, and more. You need 4–6 servings of grains each day, or 1–2 at each meal.

★ **Vegetables**—Look for colors when choosing vegetables: green ones like broccoli and spinach, red ones like red bell peppers, and orange ones like carrots and sweet potatoes. The brighter and more colorful the vegetable is, the more nutrients it has! You should eat about 2½ cups of vegetables every day.

★ **Fruits**—Fruits are nature's candy. Choose a variety that you enjoy, like grapes, watermelon, blueberries, strawberries, and more. Eating whole fruits is a better choice than drinking juice, but if you drink juice, opt for 100% juice. Aim for 1½ cups of fruit every day.

★ **Milk**—The milk group offers your body calcium, the nutrient that helps build strong bones and teeth. Dairy foods like cottage cheese, yogurt, milk, and cheese are found in this part of the pyramid. Kids should drink or eat 2–3 cups each day.

★ **Meat and Beans**—Here we get the protein we need to build our muscles and keep us strong. Beef, pork, chicken, fish, eggs, beans, and nuts are all rich sources of protein. You need about 5 ounces of protein (2 servings) each day.

★ **Sweets and Fats**—It's okay to love these foods, just keep them to a minimum. They usually don't offer much nutrition. Be smart with your choices.; 1–2 extras a day is fine, but make sure you get lots of good foods first before reaching for the sweets.

★ As far as exercise goes, try to get 60 minutes of exercise, activity, sports, or play each day. Dancing, walking, biking, skating—it all counts!

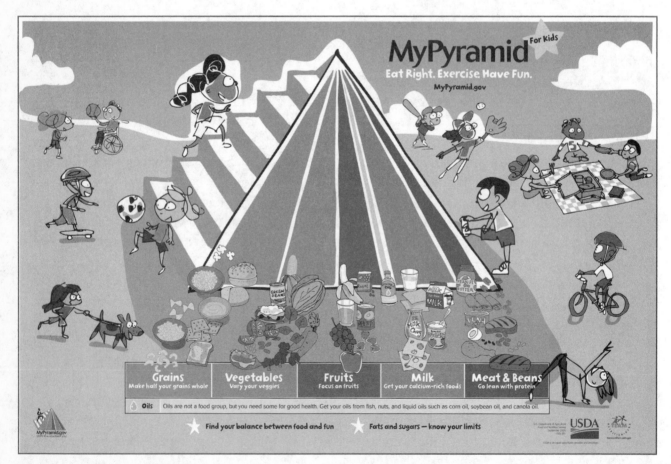

FIGURE 1-3: **MyPyramid for Kids**
The revised USDA Food Pyramid for Kids specifies what you should eat to stay healthy.

How to Read a Nutrition Label

Look on food packages for the part marked "Nutrition Facts." This section provides you with information on how much nutrition this particular food provides, as well as information about how many servings are in the package, how big a serving is, and how how many calories there are in a serving.

Looking at the Nutrition Facts food label, can you answer the following questions?

- How many calories does this food have?
- How much sugar is in this food?

The nutrients listed here are measured in what we call grams and milligrams. They're very tiny amounts, but they are very important to your body. Some vitamins and minerals are also listed by percentages, telling you how much the food gives you based on what you need each day.

Now find a Nutrition Facts label on a food package at home. Can you determine what's in the foods you eat?

FIGURE 1-4: **Nutrition Facts label**
The revised Nutrition Facts food label

Nutrition Facts

Serving Size 1 cup (228g)
Servings Per Container 2

Amount Per Serving

Calories 250   Calories from Fat 110

	% Daily Value*
Total Fat 12g	18%
Saturated Fat 3g	15%
Cholesterol 30mg	10%
Sodium 470mg	20%
Total Carbohydrate 31g	10%
Dietary Fiber 0g	0%
Sugars 5g	
Protein 5g	

Vitamin A	4%
Vitamin C	2%
Calcium	20%
Iron	4%

* Percent Daily Values are based on a 2,000 calorie diet. Your Daily Values may be higher or lower depending on your calorie needs:

		Calories	2,000	2,500
Total Fat	Less than		65g	80g
Sat Fat	Less than		20g	25g
Cholesterol	Less than		300mg	300mg
Sodium	Less than		2,400mg	2,400mg
Total Carbohydrate			300g	375g
Dietary Fiber			25g	30g

A Tasty Puzzle

You can't eat this puzzle, but you can use your "noodle"
to cook up some answers. We left you a T-A-S-T-Y hint!

ACROSS

2   This form of fat might be listed on a food label as "vegetable _____."

4   These are the parts of food that your body uses to grow, have energy, and stay healthy. Junk foods have very few of them.

8   To learn about the ingredients in your food, read the _____!

DOWN

1   You need six to eight glasses of this nutrient every day.

3   Bees make this form of sugar.

5   It's OK to have "junk food" once in a while, as a special _____.

6   Squirrels like this food, which contains a lot of protein and fat.

7   Foods at the tip of the food pyramid are loaded with fat and _____.

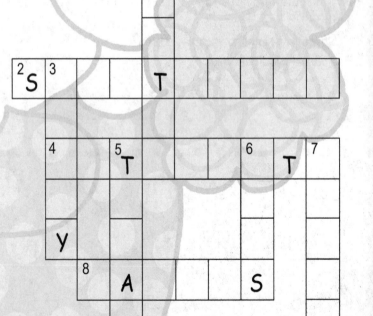

Chapter 2

Wake Up to a Good Breakfast

Breakfast is the most important meal of the day. That's because it gives you your first boost of energy for the day—enough energy to work, play, think, read, and concentrate.

The word breakfast comes from the term "breaking the fast," meaning the foods you eat break the fast from all the hours of not eating since the night before. Even though many foods are considered breakfast foods, you can eat almost anything to break that fast.

Breakfast Scrambles

First, unscramble all the words in the frying pan. Then use them to complete the riddles. HINT: These breakfast orders are silly, not normal. Think twice before you write your answers down!

SHOGT   SGEG
ASTOT   OACEBN
NBCOA   EGLS

What does a dog have for breakfast?

Woofles!

1. What does a centipede have for breakfast?

_ _ _ _ _ _ AND _ _ _ _ _

2. What does a lighthouse keeper have for breakfast?

_ _ _ _ _ _ _ AND _ _ _ _

3. What does a spook have for breakfast?

_ _ _ _ _ _ _ _ _ _

Breakfast Crepes

French crepes taste delicious with fresh fruit. Strawberries, peaches, raspberries, or blueberries make this breakfast a special treat.

▶ **DIFFICULTY: MEDIUM**

Makes 6 large crepes

3 eggs

1½ cups milk

2 tablespoons butter or
   margarine, melted

1 tablespoon sugar

½ teaspoon salt

1 cup flour

2 teaspoons oil

1 tablespoon confectioners'
   (powdered) sugar, optional

Syrup, optional

Flip It!

Flipping crepes takes some practice. You may need some help at first, or you may need to use two spatulas. Be careful!

Tip

WORDS to KNOW

Bon appetit is French for "Enjoy your meal."

1. In a large bowl, beat the eggs with a whisk.
2. Add the milk, melted butter, sugar, and salt. Mix well.
3. Add in the flour. Mix until smooth.
4. In a large skillet, heat a small amount of the oil (about 1 teaspoon) over medium heat.
5. Pour about ½ cup of the batter into the hot skillet. While holding the handle of the skillet, tilt it to spread the batter around the entire bottom of the pan.
6. Cook the crepe until the bottom begins to brown and bubbles form on the top. Use a spatula to slip the crepe over and cook the other side until it is brown, too.
7. Carefully slide the crepe out of the skillet and stack it on a plate. Continue cooking the remaining crepes until all the batter is used up. Use additional oil in the pan as needed.
8. When all the crepes are finished, roll up each crepe to serve. Add fruit or sprinkle with confectioners' sugar or syrup if you'd like.

Poppin' Popovers

Popovers are so easy to make, and they're more fun than regular muffins. You can make them in a special popover pan, a muffin pan, or even small custard cups.

▶ **DIFFICULTY:** MEDIUM

Makes 6 popovers

3 eggs
1 cup milk
3 tablespoons butter, melted
1 cup flour
Dash of salt

1. Preheat the oven to 375°F. Spray the muffin tin with cooking spray.
2. In a large bowl, beat the eggs with a whisk.
3. Add the milk, melted butter, flour, and salt. Stir until the mixture is smooth.
4. Pour the egg mixture into the prepared pan so each cup is about ⅔ full.
5. Bake 25–35 minutes, or until your popovers are puffed up and golden brown.
6. Remove popovers from pan. Serve warm or cold with butter or jam.

---

try This

CRACK AN EGG

Gently crack the eggshell on the edge of a cup or bowl; let the shell crack into two parts. Holding onto the shell, let the egg drop easily into the bowl. It's always best to crack an egg on the edge of a clear glass cup (like a glass measuring cup) or small glass bowl and drop the yolk and white into the cup or bowl before putting it together with other ingredients. That way, if the cracked egg has any eggshell in it, or if it is a bad egg that has blood or a red spot in it, you can throw it away before it ruins your other ingredients.

Cinnamon-Raisin French Toast

Serve with your favorite syrup or sprinkled with confectioners' sugar. If you can't find cinnamon raisin bread, use regular raisin bread. Make your own cinnamon flavor by adding 1 tablespoon of sugar and ½ teaspoon of cinnamon to your egg mixture.

▶ **DIFFICULTY: MEDIUM**

Makes 8 slices of French toast or 4 servings

2 eggs
⅓ cup milk
2 tablespoons butter
8 slices cinnamon raisin bread
Syrup, optional
Confectioners' (powdered) sugar, optional

1. In pie plate or large bowl, beat the eggs and milk with a whisk.
2. In large skillet, melt 1 tablespoon of the butter over medium heat.
3. Dip the slices of bread in the egg mixture, coating both sides.
4. Put 2–4 slices of bread into the heated skillet at a time, and cook 1–2 minutes on each side until golden brown. Continue with additional butter and slices of bread.

The **A**B**C**s of Kitchen Safety and Fun . . .

Ask an adult before cooking.

Bunches of Bagels

Figure out the topping on these bagels by reading the letters in a circle. The trick is to know which letter comes first, and whether to read to the right or to the left. Then decide which bagel and topping combo you would want to eat for breakfast!

Bagel #1

Bunches of Bagels

Figure out the topping on these bagels by reading the letters in a circle. The trick is to know which letter comes first, and whether to read to the right or to the left. Then decide which bagel and topping combo you would want to eat for breakfast!

Apple Cinnamon Oatmeal

You can also add raisins to this oatmeal if you would like.

▶ **DIFFICULTY: HARD**

Makes 4 servings

1 cup rolled oats (not instant)
1 cup milk
1 cup water
1 tablespoon brown sugar
1 apple, peeled and finely chopped
1 teaspoon cinnamon

1. In a large saucepan, combine the oats, milk, water, brown sugar, and chopped apple.
2. Heat the mixture over medium to high heat until it begins to boil, stirring occasionally.
3. Reduce the heat to low and let the mixture simmer for about 2–3 minutes, continuing to stir.
4. When the oatmeal thickens and gets a mushy texture to it, remove it from the heat. Pour the oatmeal into bowls and sprinkle with cinnamon before serving.

Homemade Granola

Eat granola as a snack or try it with milk for a quick, healthy breakfast cereal.

▶ **DIFFICULTY: MEDIUM**

WORDS to KNOW

molasses: the thick, brown syrup that is separated from raw sugar during the refining process.

Makes 3 cups of granola

1½ cups rolled oats (not instant)
½ cup shelled sunflower seeds
½ cup raisins or dried cranberries
¼ cup chopped walnuts
2 tablespoons melted butter
1 tablespoon oil
1 tablespoon molasses
2 tablespoons light corn syrup

1. Preheat the oven to 375°F.
2. In a large bowl, combine the oats, sunflower seeds, raisins or cranberries, and nuts.
3. In a small bowl, combine the melted butter, oil, molasses, and corn syrup.
4. Pour the butter mixture over the oat mixture and stir it well.
5. Spread the granola into a 9" × 13" baking pan. Bake 10 minutes.
6. While the granola is cooking, stir the mixture 1–2 times to help it dry out and keep it from burning.
7. Remove the granola from the oven and stir it again. Let it cool before eating. Store granola in an airtight container.

Cinnamon-Sugar Bread Sticks

Here's a quick and easy favorite to take on the go.

▶ **DIFFICULTY: EASY**

Makes 1 serving

1 slice bread, whole wheat or white
1½ teaspoons sugar
½ teaspoon cinnamon
Vegetable cooking spray

1. Place bread slices into a toaster or toaster oven. Toast to desired brownness.
2. Mix sugar and cinnamon together in a small resealable plastic bag.
3. Cut toasted bread into 4 or 5 strips.
4. Spray bread strips with cooking spray. Place strips into plastic bag and shake.
5. Eat right away or take your cinnamon sticks to go.

FUN FACT

What's Best for You?

Whole wheat bread is better than white bread because it has more iron, vitamins, and fiber.

What's So Funny?

Two cooks are telling each other a joke, but they are speaking in "Cooktalk." Can you figure out their secret language so you can join in the fun?

WEGGHEGGAEGGTEGG   TEGGWEGGOEGG
TEGGHEGGIEGGNEGGEGGSEGG
CEGGAEGGNEGG'TEGG   YEGGOEGGUEGG
HEGGAEGGVEGGE   FEGGOEGGREGG
BEGGREGGEEGGAEGGKEGGFEGGAEGGSEGGTEGG?

LEGGUEGGNEGGCEGGHEGG   AEGGNEGGDEGG
DEGGIEGGNEGGNEGGEEGGREGG!!

Favorite Fried Eggs

Everyone loves fried eggs. Do you know how to make them yourself?

▶ **DIFFICULTY:** MEDIUM

Makes 2 eggs or 1 serving

1 tablespoon butter
2 eggs
Salt and pepper, as desired

1. Crack eggs into a small bowl. Try to do this gently so you don't break the yolks. (If the yolks do break, go to Page 24 for Cheesy Scrambled Eggs.)
2. Melt the butter in a skillet over medium heat.
3. Pour eggs into the skillet and cook them until the whites set.
4. If you like your eggs sunny-side up, do not flip the eggs over. Cook them until the eggs are set and not runny. If you like your eggs over-easy, flip them over and cook until the other side sets.

How to Tell Eggs are Done

You can tell when the egg whites are set by their color change. The white will turn from almost clear to **opaque** white. The edges of the egg will also begin to brown.

Tip

WORDS to KNOW

opaque: cloudy; not clear or transparent

Food Trivia

Egg-ceptional facts:

- Eggs from many animals are edible, including eggs from ducks, geese, pigeons, turtles, ostriches, and even crocodiles.
- Caviar is an expensive luxury food that comes from snail eggs and the tiny black eggs of the sturgeon fish.
- In 1493, Christopher Columbus took chickens on his second voyage to the New World so the sailors would have eggs to eat during their travels.
- To tell whether an egg is raw or has been cooked, spin it on its pointed end. If it spins, it is cooked; if it falls over, it is raw.
- Since early times, people have decorated eggs to give as gifts at Easter and other times of the year.
- The world's most famous eggs were decorated by Russian jeweler Carl Fabergé. He made beautiful eggs for the Russian royal family for Easter and other special occasions. They were made with gems and precious metals like gold and silver, and today they are worth millions of dollars.

Cheesy Scrambled Eggs

Try combining several cheeses to create your own favorite cheesy eggs.

▶ **DIFFICULTY:** MEDIUM

Makes 4 eggs or 2 servings

4 eggs
¼ cup milk
½ teaspoon salt
Pinch of pepper
¼ cup shredded cheese, any type
1 tablespoon butter

1. Crack the eggs into a small bowl.
2. Use a whisk to beat the eggs until they are light yellow and mixed well.
3. Add the milk, salt, pepper, and cheese to the eggs.
4. Melt the butter in a skillet over medium heat.
5. Pour egg mixture into the heated skillet and let it cook. As the eggs start to set, use a spatula to break them up and turn them over.
6. When eggs are cooked throughout and no longer runny, remove them from the skillet and serve.

Hard-Boiled Eggs

Hard-boiled eggs are so easy to make, but many people are afraid to try to make them. Once they are cooked, they can be eaten plain, made into egg salad, or cut up on a chef's salad.

▶ **DIFFICULTY: MEDIUM**

Makes 2 servings

2 eggs

1. Place the eggs in a small saucepan. Fill the pan with enough water to cover the eggs.
2. Put the saucepan over medium to high heat and bring the water to a boil.
3. Once the water boils, reduce the temperature to low and let the water simmer for 12–15 minutes.
4. Remove the saucepan from the heat and pour cool water into the pan to cool the eggs. Keep the eggs in the cool water until they are cool enough to handle.
5. Gently crack the eggshells and peel them off.
6. You can serve the eggs whole, sliced on bread, or cut in half.

Bunches of Bagels

Figure out the topping on these bagels by reading the letters in a circle. The trick is to know which letter comes first, and whether to read to the right or to the left. Then decide which bagel and topping combo you would want to eat for breakfast!

Bagel #3

Fresh Blueberry Muffins

Great for breakfast or just as a snack, these muffins are just as much fun to eat as they are to make.

▶ **DIFFICULTY: MEDIUM**

Makes 1 dozen muffins

1½ cups fresh blueberries
⅔ cup sugar
1½ cups flour
½ teaspoon baking soda

½ teaspoon salt
⅓ cup oil
2 eggs, beaten
½ cup milk

1. Preheat oven to 375°F. Spray the muffin tin with cooking spray.
2. Put the blueberries into a colander and rinse them off.
3. In a large bowl, combine the sugar, flour, baking soda, and salt.
4. In a small bowl, combine the oil, beaten eggs, and milk.
5. Add the liquid ingredients into the dry ingredients and stir together until they are just blended. Do not overmix.
6. Fold the blueberries into the batter.
7. Pour the batter into the prepared pan so each cup is about ⅔ full.
8. Bake 18–20 minutes or until muffins are lightly browned and cooked throughout.
9. You can serve the muffins fresh from the oven! After they have cooled, cover them with waxed paper to keep them fresh.

try This

TEST TO BE SURE

To test for doneness, insert a toothpick into the center of the muffins. If the toothpick comes out clean, the muffins are done. If there is batter on the toothpick, the muffins need to cook another 1–2 minutes. Then test again with a clean toothpick.

Mini Bite-Sized Blueberry Pancakes

Watch these pancakes puff up as they cook. Make them as a week-end treat, but be sure to save the extras to reheat for breakfast during the week.

▶ **DIFFICULTY:** MEDIUM

Makes 3 dozen mini pancakes

1 cup flour
1 tablespoon sugar
1½ teaspoons baking powder
½ teaspoon baking soda
½ teaspoon salt
1 egg, lightly beaten

1 tablespoon melted margarine
1½ cups reduced fat buttermilk
½ cup fresh blueberries
3 teaspoons oil
Syrup or powdered sugar

1. In a large bowl, combine the flour, sugar, baking powder, baking soda, and salt.
2. Add the beaten egg, margarine, and buttermilk. Mix together with a whisk until smooth. Carefully fold in the blueberries.
3. In a large skillet, heat 1 teaspoon of the oil. Using a 1 table-spoon measure, drop pancake batter onto the hot skillet. You will have room for about 6 to 8 pancakes at a time.
4. Cook until the edges become brown and the batter becomes bubbly.
5. Flip pancakes over and cook until the other side is browned, too. Continue cooking the rest of the pancakes until all the batter is used up. (Add more oil to the pan as you need to.)
6. Serve pancakes with your favorite syrup or sprinkle with powdered sugar.

Play It Safe

How Do Foods Become Unsafe? Every surface contains microscopic substances called bacteria. These bacteria can be found on a person's hands, kitchen counters, utensils, sponges, and even in foods themselves. Some bacteria won't hurt people, and some are actually good, but others can cause food poisoning that can make people sick. By following safe food handling procedures, you can help keep your foods safe to eat.

Food Trivia

On average, it will take nearly 350 squirts from a cow's udder to produce one gallon of milk.

WORDS to KNOW

confectioners' sugar:
Finely powdered sugar with cornstarch added.

Bunches of Bagels

Figure out the topping on these bagels by reading the letters in a circle. The trick is to know which letter comes first, and whether to read to the right or to the left. Then decide which bagel and topping combo you would want to eat for breakfast!

Bagel #4

Chocolaty Chip Pancakes

Try these as a special treat after a sleepover. They are easy to make, and so much fun to eat!

▶ **DIFFICULTY: MEDIUM**

Makes 16 pancakes

1 cup flour	1 egg, lightly beaten
1 tablespoon sugar	2 tablespoons oil
1 teaspoon baking powder	Syrup
½ cup chocolate chips	Confectioners' (powdered)
1 cup milk	sugar, optional

1. In a large bowl, combine the flour, sugar, baking powder, and chocolate chips.
2. In a small bowl, combine the milk and the beaten egg.
3. Pour the milk mixture into the flour mixture and mix together with a whisk until smooth.
4. In a large skillet, heat half of the oil. Drop about 2 table-spoonfuls of pancake batter onto the hot skillet.
5. Cook until the edges become brown and the batter becomes bubbly.
6. Flip pancakes over and cook until the other side is browned, too. Continue cooking the rest of the pancakes until all the batter is used up. (Add more oil to the pan as you need to.)
7. Serve pancakes with your favorite syrup or sprinkled with confectioners' sugar.

Breakfast Burrito

Burritos are favorites for lunch and dinner; why not try a breakfast variation?

▶ **DIFFICULTY:** MEDIUM

Makes 1 burrito

1 teaspoon oil
1 egg, beaten
1 6" tortilla
1 tablespoon shredded Cheddar cheese
1½ teaspoon salsa

1. Heat oil in a small skillet over medium heat. Add egg and cook until done.
2. Place scrambled egg in center of tortilla. Top with cheese and salsa. Roll up and eat.
3. If you want your cheese melted, you can heat the burrito with cheese in the microwave for about 15 seconds before topping with the salsa.

Bunches of Bagels

Figure out the topping on these bagels by reading the letters in a circle. The trick is to know which letter comes first, and whether to read to the right or to the left. Then decide which bagel and topping combo you would want to eat for breakfast!

Bagel #5

S A L A G E D

What's Cookin' at Your House?

Are you a creative cook? You may decide to experiment with some of these recipes. If you try something new and everyone likes it, make notes here so you remember what you changed. You can also use this space to write down special recipes from your friends or family.

Recipe Title: ....

Makes .... servings

INGREDIENTS:

....

....

....

....

....

....

DIRECTIONS:

....

....

....

....

....

....

Chapter 3
Lunches, Sandwiches, & Brown Bag Ideas

unch time is fun time. It is your time to be creative and have fun with the foods you eat. Whether you are making a weekend lunch at home or packing a lunch for school, find foods that you like best. Try new things and experiment with old favorites. The more you are involved in selecting and preparing your lunch, the better you will like it!

Silly Slice

The letters in each column go in the squares directly below them, but not in the same order! Black squares show the spaces between words. When you have correctly filled in the grid, you will have the silly answer to the riddle.

Extra Help: Some letters have been done for you!

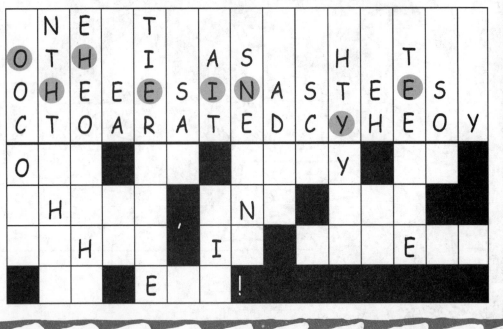

What's the difference between a person who is not smart, and a pizza?

Grilled Cheese and Tomato Sandwich

What's better than a warm and crispy grilled cheese sandwich? Here's a different spin on the old favorite that makes it more nutritious, too.

▶ **DIFFICULTY:** MEDIUM

Makes 1 sandwich

2 slices bread, white or whole wheat
1 slice American or Cheddar cheese
1–2 thin slices of tomato
1 teaspoon butter

1. Make a sandwich with the cheese and tomato between the two slices of bread.
2. Melt the butter in a small skillet over medium heat.
3. Place the sandwich in the skillet and cook it for about 2 minutes on each side, until the cheese is melted and the bread becomes slightly browned and crispy.
4. If you are making sandwiches to share, you can serve tomato or vegetable soup, too.

The **ABCs** of Kitchen Safety and Fun . . .

Clean up the kitchen as you go.

~ **Try This** ~

TOAST BREAD OR NOT

Lay 2 slices of bread side by side. Spread one with margarine and leave the other plain. Toast both slices in a toaster oven and see what happens. The plain one will toast, but the one with margarine will not. Why? Because the fat from the margarine keeps the bread moist and soft and prevents it from drying out.

City kid: Do you like raisin bread?

Farmer: Don't know; I've never raised any!

Food Trivia

The strawberry is the only agricultural product that has its seeds on the outside.

The **A**_B**C**s of Kitchen Safety and Fun . . .

Don't use sharp knives without supervision.

FUN FACT Banana Facts

A cluster of bananas is called a hand and consists of about 10–20 bananas, known as fingers. As bananas ripen, the starch inside turns to sugar; therefore, the riper the banana, the sweeter it tastes. Great Britain reported that in the year 2001 there were more than 300 banana-related accidents, most of them involving people slipping on banana peels.

Make-a-Face Sandwich

When you need a reason to play with food, try this special lunchtime treat. You can also use tuna or egg salad as the sandwich base. The possibilities are endless!

▶ **DIFFICULTY: MEDIUM**

Makes 4 halves

2 English muffins
½ cup peanut butter
1 apple, cut into slivers
4 strawberries, halved
1 banana, cut into slices

¼ cup raisins or chocolate chips
¼ cup shredded Cheddar cheese

1. Place muffin halves on a plate.
2. Wash fruit and cut it into pieces small enough to fit on an English muffin.
3. Spread peanut butter over each muffin.
4. Decorate your sandwich with any design you can think of, or try this:

   To make the face:
   - Place apple slivers to form mouth
   - Place strawberry half above apples to form nose
   - Add banana slices above the strawberry to make the eyes
   - Use raisins or chocolate chips to make eyebrows or mustache
   - Sprinkle cheese on top to make hair

5. If you have any leftover fruit, raisins, or chocolate chips, eat them on the side. These are especially fun to make with (or for) your friends!

Cheesiest Macaroni and Cheese

A popular favorite from the box—now try it from scratch! It makes a comforting warm meal or a great cold lunch.

▶ **DIFFICULTY: HARD**

Makes 4 servings

Play It Safe

Always use potholders or oven mitts to touch hot pans and dishes. You may not realize how hot something is until you've picked it up, so it's always better to start out with your hands protected.

1 cup uncooked elbow macaroni

2 tablespoons butter or margarine

2 tablespoons flour

¼ teaspoon salt

¼ teaspoon pepper

¼ teaspoon dry mustard

¼ teaspoon Worcestershire sauce

1 cup milk

1½ cups sharp Cheddar cheese, cubed or shredded

2 tablespoons seasoned breadcrumbs

1. Preheat the oven to 275°F.
2. Cook macaroni noodles in large pot of water according to package directions. Drain in a colander.
3. Melt the butter in a large saucepan over medium heat. Reduce the heat to low.
4. Add the flour, salt, pepper, mustard, and Worcestershire sauce. Stir until smooth.
5. Add the milk and cheese. Continue stirring until the cheese melts and the sauce is creamy and smooth.
6. Stir the macaroni noodles into the cheese sauce.
7. Pour the mixture into a 2-quart casserole dish. Top with the breadcrumbs.
8. Bake 30–40 minutes, or until the casserole is heated through and lightly browned. Let the casserole dish sit about 5–10 minutes before serving so the cheesy, creamy sauce has a chance to thicken.

Food Trivia

The sandwich was named for the fourth Earl of Sandwich of Britain. He created the sandwich so he could have a meal while playing a card game.

A **buffet** is a meal where many foods are set out on a table and people walk around and take what (and how much) they want.

Club It Your Way Sandwich

Set up a buffet of options for you and your guests to make sandwiches the way you like them.

▶ **DIFFICULTY: EASY**

Makes 4 sandwiches

8 slices bread, any type	½ pound deli-sliced ham
¼ cup mayonnaise	1 tomato, thinly sliced
4 lettuce leaves	4 slices cheese, any flavor
½ pound deli-sliced turkey	8 slices bacon, cooked

1. Set out the bread on a plate or in a basket.
2. Using separate small bowls or plates, set out the mayonnaise, lettuce leaves, turkey, ham, tomato slices, cheese, and bacon.
3. Create a sandwich to your own liking. Serve corn or potato chips and pickles, or look through Chapter 4 for other ideas of what to serve on the side.

Play It Safe

When Buying Food: Check expiration dates to see how long the food will be safe to store and safe to eat. When buying produce or deli foods, make sure they are fresh and have been properly refrigerated in the store. At home, store the foods at their proper temperature right away.

Mini Pizza in a Flash

Making a mini pizza is about the quickest lunch you can make. It doesn't require many ingredients, and there are so many variations to it.

▶ **DIFFICULTY: MEDIUM**

Makes 2 mini pizzas

1 English muffin or bagel, split in half

2 tablespoons pizza, spaghetti, or tomato sauce

¼ cup shredded mozzarella cheese

Meat or vegetable toppings, optional

1. Preheat the oven to 350°F.
2. Place the English muffin or bagel halves on a cookie sheet.
3. Spread the pizza sauce over each English muffin or bagel half. Top with mozzarella cheese and other toppings.
4. Bake 5–8 minutes, or until the cheese is melted.

Food Trivia

In Japan, squid is a very popular topping for pizza.

Lunch?

Start at the letter marked with the dot, and move counterclockwise. Read every other letter until you are back at the beginning. You will get the answer to this riddle: What is a mermaid's favorite lunch?

Here you are, kids!

thanks, MoM!

The **A**_B**C**s of Kitchen Safety and Fun . . .

Eat foods that are good for you.

Tasty Tuna Melt

Tuna melts make a great lunch, and they're also great to share as an afternoon snack. For a fun change, bake a potato in the microwave, top it with tuna and cheese, and bake it. You will have a Tuna Melt Potato!

▶ **DIFFICULTY: MEDIUM**

Makes 4 tuna melt sandwich halves

2 English muffins or bagels, split in half

1 6-ounce can chunk tuna in water, drained

2 tablespoons mayonnaise

¼ cup shredded or sliced cheese: Cheddar, mozzarella, or American

1. Preheat the oven to 350°F.
2. Place English muffin or bagel halves on a cookie sheet or a sheet of aluminum foil.
3. Use the can opener to open the tuna, then carefully drain the water.
4. In a small bowl, combine the drained tuna with the mayonnaise. Mix well.
5. Top each English muffin or bagel half with tuna, then with the cheese.
6. Bake 5–8 minutes, or until the cheese is melted.

What is a sheep's favorite snack?

A Baaaah-loney sandwich!

Eggy Salad

Egg salad can be used as a sandwich spread or as a dip with crackers.
Either way, it tastes so good you'll be surprised how easy it is to make.

▶ **DIFFICULTY: EASY**

Makes enough for 2 sandwiches or ½ cup dip

2 hard-boiled eggs (Page 25)
1 tablespoon mayonnaise
½ teaspoon celery salt
¼ teaspoon pepper
Paprika, optional

The **ABC**s of
Kitchen Safety and Fun . . .
Find recipes you
enjoy making.

1. Peel the shells from the hard-boiled eggs and rinse the eggs.
2. Place the eggs in a medium-sized bowl and mash with a fork or
   potato masher.
3. Add the mayonnaise, celery salt, and pepper. Mix well.
4. If you'd like, you can sprinkle paprika over the top of the egg salad.
5. Spread the egg salad over bread slices for a sandwich or place in
   a small bowl to be used as a dip with crackers, Bag of Bagel Chips
   (Page 51), or Parmesan Pita Chips (Page 53).

Food Trivia

The first microwave was introduced in the late 1940s. It was called the Radarange.

WORDS to KNOW

tortilla: a round, flat, thin cornmeal or wheat flour bread usually eaten with hot topping or filling.

Mexican Quesadillas

After trying quesadillas with just cheese, be adventurous and add some refried beans, Guacamole (Page 56), or black olives.

▶ **DIFFICULTY: EASY**

Makes 2 servings

2 flour tortillas
2 tablespoons shredded cheese, any type
Sour cream or salsa, optional

1. Place one tortilla on a large plate and sprinkle with the shredded cheese.
2. Top with the second tortilla.
3. Cook in the microwave for about 20–30 seconds, until the cheese is melted.
4. Cool slightly. Use a knife or pizza cutter to cut the tortilla into 6 wedges. Dip in sour cream or salsa, as desired.

Mystery Meal

Can you tell what this recipe will make by reading the list of ingredients? Write the name at the top of the card.

This recipe makes _____

1 cup uncooked elbow macaroni
2 tablespoons butter or margarine
2 tablespoons flour
¼ teaspoons each of salt, pepper, dry mustard, Worcestershire sauce
1 cup milk
1½ cups sharp Cheddar cheese, cubed or shredded
2 tablespoons seasoned breadcrumbs

Chicken Salad Puffs

These easy puffs may be fun to make, but they're so much more fun to eat. If you don't have leftover chicken to use here, you can either have an adult cook 2 boneless, skinless chicken breasts for you or use a 6-ounce can of chicken breast meat.

▶ **DIFFICULTY: MEDIUM**

Makes 4 servings (2 puffs each)

1 cup chopped, cooked chicken
2 tablespoons mayonnaise
¼ cup shredded Cheddar cheese
1 8-ounce package crescent rolls

1. Preheat oven to 375°F. Spray muffin pan with cooking spray.
2. Combine chopped chicken, mayonnaise, and cheese in medium bowl. Mix well.
3. Open package of crescent rolls. Press each roll into one of eight holes in the muffin pan.
4. Evenly divide chicken mixture and place into the center of each roll.
5. Cook for 10 minutes, or until golden brown and puffy.

Food Trivia

A lot of the Cheddar cheese you buy in the grocery store is orange, but that's not its natural color. Cheddar cheese is white; it only turns orange after a carrot-based food coloring is added.

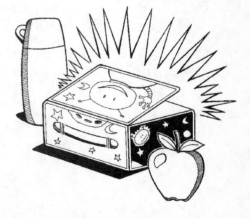

Tuna Fish and Apple Crunch Sandwich

A sweet crunch will make your tuna salad sandwich so much tastier. If you don't have an apple for this recipe, try a chopped pear.

▶ **DIFFICULTY: MEDIUM**

Makes 2 tuna sandwiches

1 16-ounce can chunk tuna in water, drained
1 small apple
1 tablespoon mayonnaise
1 pita pocket, cut in half

1. Use the can opener to open the tuna, then carefully drain the water out.
2. Peel, core, and chop apple.
3. Combine the tuna, apple, and mayonnaise in a medium bowl. Mix well.
4. Cut pita pocket in half, open up both sides, and stuff half the mixture in each pocket.

An Apple a Day

You've probably heard the saying "An apple a day keeps the doctor away." Apples are definitely good for you, but you should eat a variety of fruits and vegetables to stay healthy. What's more, the skins of apples and other foods are very good for you, so remember to leave them on whenever you can.

Tip

Tasty Tomato Soup

Tomato soup has been a family staple for years. It's just as easy to make from scratch as it is from a can.

▶ **DIFFICULTY:** HARD

Makes 4 servings

FUN FACT

Why does cutting an onion make you cry?

Onions contain a type of acid. When you peel, cut, or crush an onion, the acid is released, and that's what causes your eyes to tear up. If you don't want to cry, put the onion in the freezer for 5–10 minutes before you cut it.

10–12 ripe tomatoes
1 tablespoon oil
1 onion, chopped
3 garlic cloves, chopped

1 14½-ounce can vegetable broth
1 6-ounce can tomato paste
1 teaspoon dried basil

1. Peel and chop the tomatoes, then place them in a large bowl and set them aside.
2. In large saucepan, heat the oil over medium heat.
3. Add the onion and garlic and cook for about 3 minutes, or until the onion is tender.
4. Add the tomatoes, cover the pan, and cook for about 5 minutes to soften the tomatoes.
5. Add the vegetable broth and tomato paste.
6. Bring the mixture to a boil over high heat, then reduce it to a simmer. Cover the pan for another 10–15 minutes.
7. Pour the soup into a blender or food processor, 1 cup at a time. Do not overfill the blender. If you put too much into the blender at once, the hot liquid will overflow when you turn it on.
8. Blend the mixture until it is smooth.
9. Pour blended soup into serving bowls to serve and sprinkle with basil. Continue with remaining portions. It may be helpful to prepare this soup in advance and transfer the blended soup to a new saucepan on the stove to keep warm.

The Soup Pot

Familiar soups and soup ingredients are hiding in each row of this soup pot! To find them, put one letter from the list into each empty box. The letter might be at the beginning, middle, or end of the word. We gave you one important ingredient to get you started! HINT: Each letter on the list will be used only once.

A D H I M M N N N O O O S ☒ R R

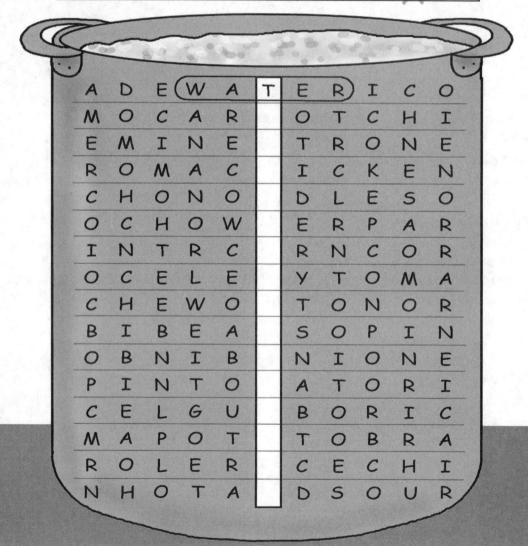

A	D	E	(W	A	T)	E	R)	I	C	O
M	O	C	A	R		O	T	C	H	I
E	M	I	N	E		T	R	O	N	E
R	O	M	A	C		I	C	K	E	N
C	H	O	N	O		D	L	E	S	O
O	C	H	O	W		E	R	P	A	R
I	N	T	R	C		R	N	C	O	R
O	C	E	L	E		Y	T	O	M	A
C	H	E	W	O		T	O	N	O	R
B	I	B	E	A		S	O	P	I	N
O	B	N	I	B		N	I	O	N	E
P	I	N	T	O		A	T	O	R	I
C	E	L	G	U		B	O	R	I	C
M	A	P	O	T		T	O	B	R	A
R	O	L	E	R		C	E	C	H	I
N	H	O	T	A		D	S	O	U	R

44

Creamy Corn Chowder

This hearty soup makes a cozy meal on a cold day.

▶ **DIFFICULTY:** HARD

Makes 6 servings

~ **Try This** ~

IS IT DONE YET?

To test potatoes for doneness, insert a fork into a few
different cooked potatoes. If
the fork goes in easily, they
are done.

1 tablespoon oil

1 onion, finely chopped

3 medium potatoes, peeled
  and chopped

2 cups water

½ teaspoon salt

¼ teaspoon pepper

2 tablespoons cornstarch

2 15¼-ounce cans corn,
  drained

2 cups milk

2 tablespoons butter or
  margarine

1. In a large saucepan, heat the oil over medium heat.
2. Add the onion and cook for about 5 minutes, stirring frequently.
3. Add the potatoes, water, salt, and pepper.
4. Turn up the heat until the mixture begins to boil.
5. When the soup starts to boil, reduce it to a simmer and continue to cook for about 20 minutes, or until the potatoes are tender.
6. In a separate bowl, mix the cornstarch with a little warm water to avoid clumps.
7. Add the corn, milk, and butter to the soup. Stir in the cornstarch to help thicken the soup.
8. Continue simmering for another 20 minutes, stirring occasionally.
9. Cool slightly before serving. Try your chowder with a salad and fruit for a complete meal.

What's Cookin' at Your House?

Are you a creative cook? You may decide to experiment with some of these recipes. If you try something new and everyone likes it, make notes here so you remember what you changed. You can also use this space to write down special recipes from your friends or family.

Recipe Title: ....

Makes .... servings

INGREDIENTS:

....

....

....

....

....

....

DIRECTIONS:

....

....

....

....

....

....

Chapter 4

Snack Time

Most people love to eat snacks, whether they are an after-school treat or a before-dinner **appetizer**.

Sharing Snacks

Making and sharing snacks is one way you can express your creativity. Snacks should satisfy those hunger pangs and carry you on to the next meal. With some imagination and ingredients you might already have at home, you can have fun today and snack well tomorrow, too!

Chips and Dip

Fill in all the triangles to find the answer to this question:

What's the most popular dip in the United States?

Oh boy — my favorite!

Peanut Butter Chip Muffins

For a different twist, you can substitute ¼ cup of chocolate chips for ¼ cup of the peanut butter chips.

▶ **DIFFICULTY:** MEDIUM

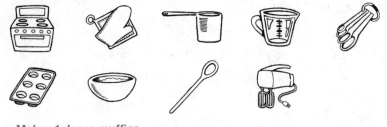

Makes 1 dozen muffins

WORDS to KNOW

appetizer: a food or drink that stimulates the appetite and is usually served before a meal.

1 cup smooth peanut butter	1½ cups flour
1 egg	1 tablespoon baking powder
¼ cup sugar	½ cup peanut butter chips
¼ cup brown sugar	Chocolate icing or melted
1 cup milk	chocolate, optional

1. Preheat oven to 375°F. Spray a muffin pan with cooking spray or line the cups with paper liners.
2. In a bowl, combine the peanut butter, egg, sugar, brown sugar, and milk, using an electric mixer to beat the ingredients until smooth.
3. Add the flour and baking powder. Mix until just blended. Do not overmix.
4. Stir in the peanut butter chips.
5. Pour the batter into the prepared muffin pan so each cup is about ⅔ full.
6. Bake for 15 minutes or until the muffins are light brown on top. Cool the muffins in the pan before removing them.

Play It Safe

Get all ingredients out before you start to cook so you don't have to hunt down any ingredients while you are in the middle of a recipe.

Food Trivia

It takes about 550 peanuts to make a 12-ounce jar of peanut butter.

Nutty Caramel Corn

A fun snack for the fall, this fan favorite is commonly seen around Halloween. Try it along with some caramel apples, and you will have a party.

▶ **DIFFICULTY: HARD**

Makes about 6 cups

1 3½-ounce bag plain microwave popcorn, popped
1 cup dry-roasted, salted peanuts
1 cup brown sugar
½ cup (1 stick) butter
½ cup corn syrup
¼ teaspoon salt

1. Preheat the oven to 200°F. Spray a 9" × 13" baking pan with cooking spray.
2. In a large bowl, combine the popped popcorn and nuts.
3. In a medium saucepan, combine the brown sugar, butter, corn syrup, and salt.
4. Heat over medium to high heat until mixture is melted and smooth, stirring constantly. This should take 4–5 minutes.
5. Remove from heat and pour caramel mixture over the popcorn and nuts, mixing well.
6. Spread out the popcorn mixture on the prepared baking pan.
7. Bake 1 hour, stirring every 15 minutes.

Quick-Eating S'mores

You don't need a campfire to make this all-time favorite outdoor snack. Here's a quick version that's good any time of the year, any time of the day or night.

▶ **DIFFICULTY:** EASY

Makes 1 S'more

1 large marshmallow
1 chocolate bar square
2 graham cracker squares

1. Place the marshmallow and chocolate bar square between the 2 graham cracker squares to make a "sandwich."
2. Place your "sandwich" on a plate and cover with a paper towel.
3. Cook for 10 seconds in the microwave, until the marshmallow puffs and melts slightly.

Bag of Bagel Chips

Hard, day-old bagels work great for this recipe. Try using cinnamon raisin, blueberry, or other fruited flavors for a sweeter chip.

▶ **DIFFICULTY:** HARD

Makes about 20–24 bagel chips

3–4 leftover bagels, 1–2 days old

1. Preheat the oven to 350°F.
2. Slice the bagel in thin circle slices (like chips), about ¼" thick each.
3. Lay the bagel slices onto a cookie sheet. Place the cookie sheet in the oven and bake for 10–12 minutes, or until the bagel slices are lightly browned and crispy. Keep cooled bagel chips in an airtight container and grab them for a quick snack.

Leftovers

Take a word from column B and write it next to a word in column A to make the name of a familiar food. There is more than one way to match up some words—make sure there are no leftovers!

COLUMN A	COLUMN B
CUP _____	*FRIES*
STRAW _____	*MELT*
POTATO _____	*SAUCE*
PEANUT _____	*ROLL*
POP _____	*BURGER*
CORN _____	*BERRY*
COLE _____	*CORN*
HOT _____	*BUTTER*
HAM _____	*CAKE*
FRENCH _____	*SALAD*
TUNA _____	*SLAW*
APPLE _____	*CHIPS*
EGG _____	*DOG*

Parmesan Pita Chips

You can serve your pita chips with a dip or hummus or store them in an airtight container for snacking any time.

▶ **DIFFICULTY: MEDIUM**

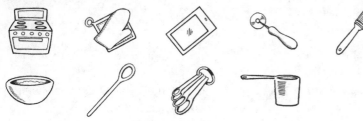

hummus: A Middle Eastern dish that is a mixture of mashed chickpeas, garlic, and other ingredients, used especially as a dip for pita.

Makes about 4 dozen pita chips

4 pieces pita bread
½ cup grated Parmesan cheese
1½ tablespoons sesame seeds
6 tablespoons oil

1. Preheat the oven to 425°F.
2. Split each pita bread in half, then use a pizza cutter to cut each half into 3 wedges.
3. Place wedges on a cookie sheet.
4. In a small bowl, combine the Parmesan cheese and sesame seeds.
5. Brush the oil on the top of each pita wedge.
6. Sprinkle pita wedges with Parmesan-sesame mixture.
7. Bake 5–10 minutes, or until light brown.

Take-Along Trail Mix

Trail mix is so versatile you can create your own versions, too. Try adding some yogurt-covered raisins, dry cereal, fish crackers, chocolate-coated candies, or even popcorn.

▶ **DIFFICULTY: EASY**

Makes 2 cups of trail mix

½ cup small pretzel sticks or twists
½ cup raisins
½ cup peanuts
¼ cup sunflower seeds
¼ cup chocolate chips

1. In a large bowl, combine all ingredients together. Store in an airtight container or resealable bag.

Answer the questions about this bag of snack mix!

Sorting the Snacks

- How many different kinds of snacks are there?
- Of which snack is there only one?
- Are there more pieces of popcorn or jelly beans?

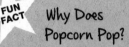

Never-Enough Nachos

For a quick vegetarian version, try making this without the beef. You can enjoy it as a snack with friends or even as an appetizer before a family meal.

▶ **DIFFICULTY:** HARD

Makes 8–10 servings

1 pound ground beef	2 cups tortilla chips
1 cup prepared salsa	½ cup sour cream
1 medium tomato	1 cup shredded Cheddar
4 green onions	cheese
½ cup lettuce	

1. Heat the oven to 350°F.
2. In a large skillet, cook the ground beef for 8–10 minutes, until it is cooked throughout. Drain the ground beef, then place it in a large bowl.
3. Add the salsa and mix well.
4. Chop the tomatoes and onion (or get an adult to help), and chop lettuce into small pieces. Place in separate small bowls.
5. In a 2-quart casserole, layer the ground beef and the other ingredients, starting at the bottom:

   - Tortilla chips
   - Ground beef
   - Sour cream
   - Tomatoes
   - Onions
   - Lettuce
   - Shredded cheese

6. Bake 20–30 minutes, or until the cheese completely melts.

FUN FACT

Why Does Popcorn Pop?

Each popcorn kernel contains a small drop of water stored inside. When the kernel gets heated, the water inside turns to steam. The kernel then begins to expand as pressure starts to develop inside the hard shell. As a result, the kernel splits open and the popcorn explodes, popping the popcorn and releasing the steam. (Popcorn is a special breed of corn. You cannot take a regular corn kernel and make it pop.)

Peel, Pit, and Mash an Avocado

Use a knife to pull the peel away from a *ripe* avocado—it should easily come off—then cut in half and remove the pit. Place the avocado in a bowl and use a fork or potato masher to mash until it's smooth.

Tip

WORDS to KNOW

ripe: fully developed and ready to be eaten.

pitted: Without the center pit (as in peaches, olives, or avocados)

Guacamole Dip with Tortillas

You can also use your guacamole with Never-Enough Nachos (Page 55) or with your favorite southwestern-style food, including quesadillas, burritos, and tacos.

▶ **DIFFICULTY: EASY**

Makes about 1½ cups of guacamole

1 plum tomato, chopped
2 ripe avocados, peeled, pitted, and mashed
1 tablespoon chopped onion
1 tablespoon lime juice
1 teaspoon chopped garlic
¼ teaspoon salt
Dash of pepper
Tortilla chips

1. Chop the tomato (or get someone to help you). Place the chopped tomato in a medium bowl.
2. Add remaining ingredients and mix well.

Chocolate Chip Granola

Not only is this fun to eat by itself, it makes a great topping for yogurt and ice cream.

▶ **DIFFICULTY: MEDIUM**

Makes 5 cups of granola

3½ cups rolled oats (not instant)
¼ cup oil
¼ cup honey
1 teaspoon vanilla
½ cup chocolate chips
½ cup white chocolate chips
½ cup sunflower seeds
½ cup slivered almonds

1. Preheat the oven to 300°F and spray a 9" × 13" baking pan with cooking spray.
2. In a large bowl, combine all ingredients and mix well.
3. Spread out granola mixture in the prepared pan.
4. Bake 15–20 minutes, or until lightly browned and heated throughout. Store cooled granola in an airtight container.

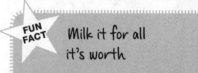

FUN FACT Milk it for all it's worth

The average American drinks twenty-five gallons of milk every year.

Chocolate C

Food Trivia

Nuts are actually a dry type of fruit that grow in a hard shell.

Cinnamon Apples to Go

When you take these to go, remember to grab a napkin. You will enjoy eating them so much, you will lick your fingers clean.

▶ **DIFFICULTY: MEDIUM**

Makes 1 serving

1 apple, any variety
1 teaspoon sugar
½ teaspoon cinnamon

1. Peel apple. Remove seeds and cut into thin slices. Place apple slices into a small resealable plastic bag.
2. Measure sugar and cinnamon and put into bag over apples.
3. Shake your bag. Take your apples to go.

The Apple Barrel

Marco, Jake, Ben, and Ethan are best friends who share everything. Today they went apple picking and came home with thirteen apples. Some of the apples are really big and some are pretty tiny. How can the four boys divide the apples evenly if they don't have a scale with which to weigh them?

Lickity-Split Fruity Banana Split

You can substitute fresh fruit, like strawberries and blueberries, or other canned fruits like peaches if you like.

▶ **DIFFICULTY: EASY**

Makes 1 serving

1 small banana
½ cup cottage cheese
¼ cup canned mandarin
   oranges, drained

¼ cup pineapple chunks or
   tidbits, drained
Colored sprinkles
1 maraschino cherry

1. Peel banana and slice in half lengthwise. Place banana halves on a plate.
2. Spoon the cottage cheese down the center of the banana.
3. Top with oranges and pineapple.
4. Shake sprinkles over the top of the cottage cheese and top with the cherry.

FUN FACT **In the Beginning**

The banana split was created in the early 1900s in Pennsylvania by a pharmacist concocting soda fountain treats.

Pudding in a Cone

What a fun and different snack! You will love to eat your pudding in a cone—just like ice cream! If you don't plan to eat the pudding right away, don't put it into the cones. If the cones sit too long, they will get soft and soggy.

▶ **DIFFICULTY: EASY**

Makes 6 servings

1 4-ounce package instant
   pudding
2 cups milk

6 small cake ice cream cones
Assorted sprinkles

1. Prepare pudding mix according to package directions.
2. Scoop pudding into ice cream cones. Decorate with assorted sprinkles. Set cones into cups, glasses, or muffin tin and place in refrigerator until set, about 10–15 minutes. Eat immediately.

What's Cookin' at Your House?

Are you a creative cook? You may decide to experiment with some of these recipes. If you try something new and everyone likes it, make notes here so you remember what you changed. You can also use this space to write down special recipes from your friends or family.

Recipe Title: ....

Makes .... servings

INGREDIENTS:

....

....

....

....

....

....

DIRECTIONS:

....

....

....

....

....

....

Chapter 5

What's for Dinner?

Along time ago, dinnertime was always family time. Many families are trying to spend meals together again because it's the one time during the day when everyone is sitting in the same place!

During family dinners, have a good conversation with your parents and siblings and eat a good meal, too. If dinner is a busy time in your house, offer to help and use these great dinner ideas.

Chef Andrew

Andrew has cooked his very first meal all by himself. What did he make? Use the picture and letter equations to sound out the answers!

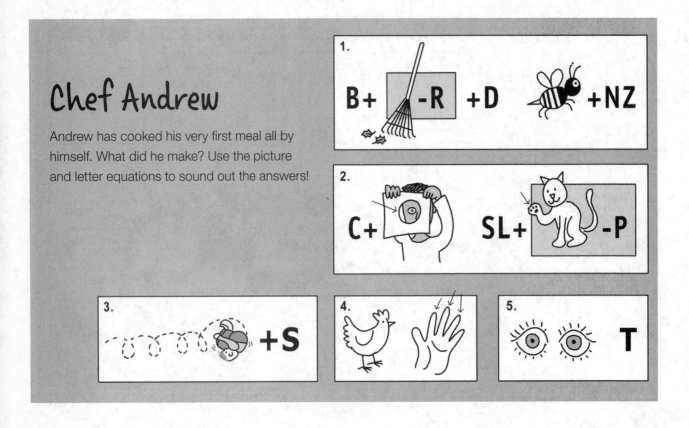

Not-So-Messy Sloppy Joes

To make these easier—and not so messy—to eat, scoop out a small amount of bread from the bun to make a well. Put the Sloppy Joes in the well and top with the other half of the bun. It works!

▶ **DIFFICULTY: HARD**

Makes 8 servings

1 pound ground beef
1 onion, chopped
2 cups frozen hash brown potatoes
1 15½-ounce can Sloppy Joe sauce
8 hamburger buns

Play It Safe

Handling Leftovers: Keep leftovers in a bowl sealed tightly with plastic wrap or in airtight containers. Promptly store them in the freezer or refrigerator.

1. In a large skillet, brown the ground beef. Drain the extra fat from the ground beef.
2. Add the onions and potatoes.
3. Pour the Sloppy Joe sauce over the top, stirring to blend the ingredients. Cover the skillet.
4. Reduce the heat to low and simmer for 30 minutes.

Tasty Tacos

Everyone loves tacos in some form or another. Add some Guacamole (Page 56) and sour cream, or even substitute soft shells for a change.

▶ **DIFFICULTY: HARD**

Makes 8 tacos

1 pound ground beef
1 tablespoon taco seasoning
2 tablespoons water
1 tomato, chopped
½ cup shredded lettuce
½ cup shredded Cheddar cheese
½ cup salsa
8 hard taco shells

1. In a large skillet, brown the ground beef. Drain the excess fat from the ground beef.
2. Add the taco seasoning and water. Stir well.
3. Put the ground beef mixture into a serving bowl.
4. Put the chopped tomato, shredded lettuce, shredded cheese, and salsa in separate serving bowls.
5. Serve with the ground beef and taco shells.

Play It Safe

Be sure to wash your hands with soap and water before touching food. It is also important to wash your hands right after you handle raw meat or fish, before you touch other things.

Crispy, Crunchy Chicken Legs

These are great for dinner, but they also taste great cold. Save some for your lunch box tomorrow.

▶ **DIFFICULTY:** MEDIUM

Makes 4 chicken legs

½ cup milk

1 cup corn flake crumbs

1 tablespoon flour

½ teaspoon paprika

½ teaspoon salt

¼ teaspoon pepper

4 chicken legs

1. Preheat the oven to 375°F.
2. Pour the milk into one flat pie plate.
3. In another flat pie plate or shallow bowl, combine the corn flake crumbs with flour and spices.
4. Roll the chicken legs first in the milk and then in the crumbs to coat them well.
5. Place chicken legs into a baking pan.
6. Bake for 35–45 minutes, or until the chicken legs are fully cooked.

Play It Safe

To test for doneness, cut into the chicken and see if the chicken is white on the inside. If there is any pink, the chicken is not fully cooked and needs to cook for a few more minutes.

pie plate: Shallow dish made of glass or metal, used for making pies. Because it is shallow, it is also widely used for dipping and rolling foods, such as coating chicken with crumbs.

~try This~

Make your own bread crumbs by putting corn flakes or toasted, dried bread in a resealable bag and smashing them with a rolling pin until they are all crumbs.

Parmesan Chicken Fingers

Making your own chicken fingers is so easy, you will wonder why you didn't try to make them before. And this recipe lets you add some Parmesan cheese to make them even tastier.

▶ **DIFFICULTY: HARD**

Serves 4

2 boneless, skinless chicken breasts
1 egg, beaten
¼ cup milk
1 tablespoon oil
1 tablespoon water
½ cup bread crumbs

¼ cup grated Parmesan cheese
2 tablespoons flour
½ teaspoon salt
¼ teaspoon pepper
2 tablespoons oil

1. Cut the chicken breasts into slices or chunks. Set aside in a large bowl.
2. In a small bowl, combine the beaten egg, milk, 1 tablespoon of oil, and water. Pour over the chicken.
3. In a flat pie plate, combine the bread crumbs, Parmesan cheese, flour, salt, and pepper. Mix together.
4. Remove the chicken fingers from the liquid mixture and dip into the bread crumb mixture, coating evenly.
5. Set the chicken fingers onto a plate or a sheet of waxed paper.
6. In a large skillet, heat 2 tablespoons of oil. Cook the chicken fingers in the hot oil until they are lightly browned, turning and flipping chicken fingers as necessary until they are fully cooked.

Chicken Quesadillas with Salsa

This recipe is easy enough that you will be able to make it for yourself and your family. Try it with different kinds of cheeses and even add some vegetables if you like.

▶ **DIFFICULTY:** MEDIUM

Makes 2 quesadillas

4 tortillas
½ cup chopped, cooked chicken (leftover chicken works great)
¼ cup Cheddar cheese
2 tablespoons salsa

1. Place 1 tortilla on a microwave-safe dinner plate.
2. Top with half of the cooked chicken and half of the cheese. Place another tortilla on top.
3. Heat quesadilla in microwave for 15–20 seconds, or until the cheese melts. Cool slightly, then cut into wedges to serve.
4. Repeat with remaining ingredients.

Food Trivia

The average American eats more than 80 pounds of chicken each year.

Orange Chicken

If you don't like onions, just take them off the chicken before serving.

▶ **DIFFICULTY: HARD**

Makes 4 servings

4 skinless, boneless chicken breasts
4 teaspoons Dijon-flavored mustard
2 green onions, chopped
¾ cup orange juice
2 teaspoons butter or margarine
3 tablespoons brown sugar

1. Preheat the oven to 350°F.
2. Place the chicken in a 9" × 13" baking dish.
3. Spread the mustard and onion pieces evenly over the chicken breasts.
4. Pour the orange juice into the dish around and over the chicken. (No basting required.)
5. Top each chicken breast with dots of butter and sprinkle with the brown sugar.
6. Bake uncovered for 30–35 minutes, or until chicken is fully cooked.

WORDS to KNOW

basting: to moisten at intervals with a liquid (such as melted butter or pan drippings) during cooking

Cheese-Crusted Fish Fillets

You can start with either frozen or fresh fish fillets, depending on what you have in your refrigerator or freezer. Whitefish, turbot, and orange roughy are all types of fish that work great with this recipe.

▶ **DIFFICULTY: HARD**

Makes 4 servings

1 pound fish fillets

1 4-ounce package softened cream cheese

1 garlic clove, minced

2 green onions, chopped

1 teaspoon lemon juice

1 tablespoon chopped parsley

1. Preheat oven to 350°F. Spray a 9" × 13" baking pan with cooking spray.
2. Lay the fish fillets in a single layer in the baking pan.
3. In a small bowl, combine the cream cheese, garlic, green onions, and lemon juice. Mix well.
4. Spread the cream cheese mixture over the top of each fish fillet.
5. Bake for 35–40 minutes, or until the fish is lightly browned on top and fully cooked. Sprinkle with parsley before serving.

Play It Safe

You have to test baked fish to make sure it's done. With a fork, pick off a piece from the end of the fish when you think it might be done cooking. If the fish flakes off easily, it is done. If it doesn't come off easily, cook it for a few minutes longer and repeat the process.

Food Trivia

There are more than 30,000 kinds of fish in the earth's waters.

Oven-Fried Fish

If you enjoy the taste of frozen fish sticks, here's an option that is just as easy to make—and a whole lot healthier, too. Orange roughy, cod, and catfish are all types of fish that work well with this recipe.

▶ **DIFFICULTY: MEDIUM**

Makes 4 servings

½ cup milk
½ cup seasoned bread crumbs
2 tablespoons grated Parmesan cheese
1 pound fish fillets

1. Preheat oven to 350°F. Spray a 9" × 13" baking pan with cooking spray.
2. Put the milk in a flat pie plate or shallow bowl.
3. In another flat pie plate, combine the bread crumbs and Parmesan cheese.
4. Dip the fish into the milk and then into the bread crumb mixture.
5. Place the fish into the prepared baking pan.
6. Bake for 20–25 minutes, or until fully cooked. Serve on buns with lettuce and sliced tomatoes.

Tuna Noodle Casserole

This classic is an old, familiar "comfort food." It makes you feel so good when you eat it, and the leftovers taste as good as the original meal.

▶ **DIFFICULTY:** MEDIUM

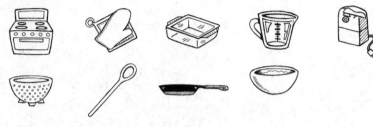

Makes 6–8 servings

8 ounces egg noodles

1 10¾-ounce can cream of mushroom soup

1 cup milk

2 6-ounce cans tuna fish in water, drained

¼ cup fried onions, for topping

1. Preheat the oven to 375°F. Spray a 2-quart casserole dish with cooking spray.
2. Prepare the egg noodles according to package directions. Drain.
3. In large bowl, combine the cooked noodles, mushroom soup, milk, and drained tuna. Mix well.
4. Pour the tuna noodle mixture into the prepared casserole dish. Sprinkle the top of the casserole with fried onions.
5. Bake for 25–30 minutes. (If the onions start to get too brown, cover the casserole dish with aluminum foil until it is done cooking.) Let the casserole dish cool slightly before serving.

FUN FACT

How much pasta do we eat?

According to the National Pasta Association, the average person in North America eats about 15½ pounds of pasta each year—but that's nothing compared to our European friends in the boot-shaped peninsula. The average Italian eats more than 51 pounds of pasta every year.

Bite-Sized Pizza

These pizzas can be made in a flash when time is limited. Keep the ingredients on hand, and you can have them ready in less than 20 minutes. Experiment with some veggie toppings, too.

▶ **DIFFICULTY: MEDIUM**

Makes 10 mini pizzas

1 can refrigerated biscuits
¾ cup pasta sauce
¾ cup shredded mozzarella cheese

Oodles of Noodles

Follow the strands of linguini over and under to see which kid gets which meatball.

1. Preheat the oven to 375°F.
2. Open biscuit can and separate biscuits.
3. Flatten out each of the biscuits onto a cookie sheet.
4. Using a large spoon, spread about 1 tablespoon of the pasta sauce over each biscuit. Top with about 1 tablespoon of the mozzarella cheese.
5. Bake pizzas for 8–10 minutes, or until crusts are golden brown and cheese is melted.

Fettuccine Alfredo with Chicken (or Not)

It's no secret that kids love pasta with Alfredo sauce. Here's an option to make at home. Make it with chicken or not, add a tossed salad and some fruit on the side, and your dinner is complete.

▶ **DIFFICULTY: HARD**

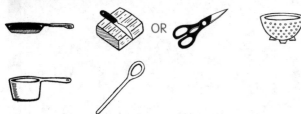

Makes 4 servings

2 boneless, skinless chicken breasts
½ pound uncooked fettuccine noodles
¼ cup half-and-half
½ cup evaporated skim milk
2 teaspoons butter or margarine
¾ cup grated Parmesan cheese
Basil, optional

1. In a small skillet, cook chicken breasts until done. Cool slightly, then cut up into strips. Set aside.
2. Prepare fettuccine according to package directions. Drain.
3. In a large saucepan, combine half-and-half, milk, and butter. Heat over medium heat until butter is melted and the mixture is hot. Slowly add in the Parmesan cheese.
4. Reduce the heat to low and cook until the cheese is blended and the mixture begins to get thick.
5. Stir in the fettuccine and the chicken. If desired, add basil before serving.

Play It Safe

Know how to use the various appliances and utensils you will need. If you need to, ask an adult to teach or remind you, especially if you are using anything with hot oil (like a wok) or sharp moving parts (like a food processor).

What's Cookin' at Your House?

Are you a creative cook? You may decide to experiment with some of these recipes. If you try something new and everyone likes it, make notes here so you remember what you changed. You can also use this space to write down special recipes from your friends or family.

Recipe Title: ....

Makes ....servings

INGREDIENTS:

....

....

....

....

....

....

DIRECTIONS:

....

....

....

....

....

....

Chapter 6

Get in Your Greens

ating fruits and vegetables every day helps you balance your meals and give you the nutrition you need to stay healthy. When you choose a vegetable or a fruit think about all the different colors to choose from—the more colorful you make your plate, the more nutrients you are adding to your overall diet. Opt for some orange (carrots and sweet potatoes), red (red bell peppers and tomatoes), and some green (broccoli and spinach) to help you grow and stay healthy. See how many different choices you can find.

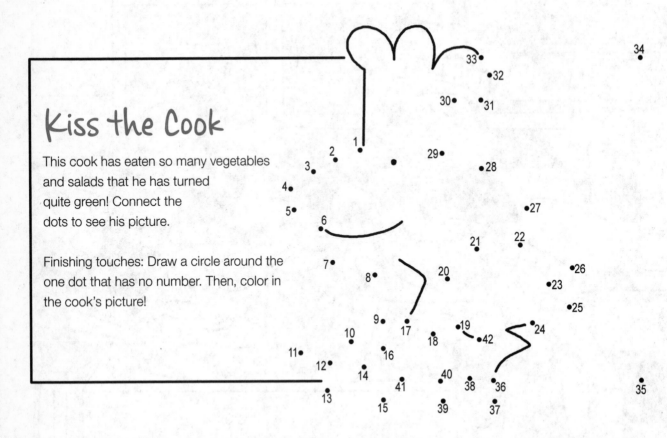

Kiss the Cook

This cook has eaten so many vegetables and salads that he has turned quite green! Connect the dots to see his picture.

Finishing touches: Draw a circle around the one dot that has no number. Then, color in the cook's picture!

Waldorf Salad

This salad was named after the Waldorf-Astoria Hotel in New York City where it was first made. Now there are so many versions of it, it has become a famous-named salad.

▶ **DIFFICULTY:** MEDIUM

Makes 4 servings

1 large red apple
2 stalks celery
2 tablespoons nuts
2 tablespoons raisins
1 teaspoon lemon juice
2 tablespoons mayonnaise

1. Chop the apple, celery, and nuts into ½" chunks. (If you don't have an apple corer, ask an adult to help you get the stem and seeds out of the apple.)
2. Combine all of the ingredients in a large bowl. Mix well.
3. Keep the salad refrigerated until you are ready to serve it.

Keep your foods from turning brown

When you cut up fresh fruits like apples and bananas, add a little orange juice or lemon juice to the fruit. The acid in the juice helps keep the fruit from turning brown after it is exposed to the air.

WORDS to KNOW

colander: a pan or bowl that has a lot of little holes in it, used for draining liquids

FUN FACT

Where did lettuce first come from?

Lettuce has been around since the times of ancient Greece and Rome. Persian rulers grew it more than 2,500 years ago.

Classic Caesar Salad

Caesar salad is light and fresh, and in addition to being a meal by itself, it goes very well with simple dinners like grilled steak or Italian foods like Fettuccine Alfredo (Page 73).

▶ **DIFFICULTY: EASY**

Makes 2 servings

1 small bunch romaine lettuce, or about 2 cups torn up
2 tablespoons freshly shredded Parmesan cheese
½ cup croutons
2 tablespoons bottled Caesar salad dressing

1. Wash the romaine lettuce.
2. Tear the lettuce into small pieces and place it into a large bowl.
3. Top with Parmesan cheese and croutons.
4. Using serving utensils, toss salad dressing into the salad and serve immediately.

Lemon and Honey Dressing

This dressing is a perfect sauce for baked chicken or fish. You can use it as a marinade or pour over the meat once cooked.

▶ **DIFFICULTY: EASY**

Yields 2 servings; serving size ¼ cup

1 small bunch romaine lettuce, or about 2 cups torn up
¼ cup lemon juice

⅓ cup honey
¼ teaspoon nutmeg
¼ teaspoon salt

1. Wash the romaine lettuce.
2. Tear the lettuce into small pieces and place it into a large bowl.
3. Mix lemon juice and honey in a small bowl.
4. Add the nutmeg and salt and continue to whisk briskly.
5. Serve over salad.

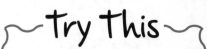

try This

MAKE YOUR OWN SALAD DRESSING

Take an empty salad dressing bottle or a small glass jar with a lid. Pour ¼ cup of vinegar and ¾ cup oil into the bottle. Add a little bit of salt and pepper, screw on the lid, and shake. Voilà! You have your own salad dressing. You can experiment with different types of vinegar and oil and add your favorite herbs to create a salad dressing like no other.

Hidden Veggies

Find six vegetables from the list hiding in the sentences.

1. Chop each carrot very carefully!
2. Abe answered "I love lettuce!"
3. Can you spin a cherry?
4. Fill the cab! Bag each vegetable!
5. The bee tasted the broccoli.

TOMATO
SPINACH
PEPPER
CABBAGE
CELERY
TURNIP
PEA
BEAN
BEET

~try This~

Visit a local farm or, better yet, plant some string bean plants in your backyard garden. You can watch the string beans grow and pick them yourself. Then, you can add your own homegrown string beans to dinner.

Green Beans with Almonds

There's nothing like the fresh, crisp sound of snapping beans. This recipe is not only fun and easy to make, but crunchy and healthy to eat.

▶ **DIFFICULTY:** MEDIUM

Makes 4 servings

½ pound fresh green beans
1 tablespoon butter or margarine
¼ cup slivered almonds
½ teaspoon salt
¼ teaspoon pepper

1. Trim the beans by snapping off the ends and removing any loose strings, then use a colander to hold the beans while you wash them in cool water.
2. In a large saucepan, heat 2 quarts of water to boiling.
3. Add the beans to the boiling water. Cook them for about 5 minutes, until they are slightly tender but still crisp.
4. Drain the green beans and return them to the saucepan.
5. Add the butter, almonds, salt, and pepper, and toss them until the butter is melted and the green beans are evenly coated.

Sweetened Baby Carrots

Baby carrots are made from full-sized carrots, but they're peeled and cut into smaller pieces to be more appealing. You can enjoy them raw or cooked, like this recipe.

▶ **DIFFICULTY: MEDIUM**

Makes 4 servings

1 pound baby carrots
1 tablespoon butter or margarine
2 tablespoons brown sugar

1. In a large saucepan, combine the carrots and just enough water to cover them.
2. Put the saucepan over high heat until the water begins to boil.
3. Reduce the heat to medium and continue cooking until the carrots are slightly tender, about 15 minutes.
4. Using a colander, drain the carrots and return them to the saucepan.
5. Add the butter and brown sugar to the saucepan, stirring until the butter is melted and the carrots are well coated.

Surprise Salad

Find eleven items in Rebecca's salad before they get eaten!

BICYCLE   DIAMOND RING
KITE   CHRISTMAS TREE
BALLOON
BELL
HEART
SAIL BOAT
MITTEN
CROWN
GHOST

Sweet Potato Casserole

Serve this warm, sweet side dish as a special treat at any holiday meal.

▶ **DIFFICULTY:** MEDIUM

Makes 6 servings

2 17-ounce cans sweet potatoes, drained and mashed
1½ cups mini marshmallows, divided into 1 cup and ½ cup
   portions
¼ cup margarine, melted
¼ cup orange juice
½ teaspoon cinnamon

1. Preheat the oven to 350°F.
2. In a large bowl, mash the drained sweet potatoes until they are mostly smooth.
3. Add 1 cup marshmallows, margarine, orange juice, and cinnamon. Gently mix them together.
4. Pour the mixture into a 1-quart casserole dish.
5. Bake 20 minutes.
6. Sprinkle the remaining marshmallows over the top of the casserole and return to the oven for 5 minutes longer.

FUN FACT

Where do sweet potatoes come from?

Sweet potatoes have been around longer than the United States. Native Americans grew sweet potatoes and introduced them to European settlers. George Washington grew sweet potatoes at Mount Vernon, his home in Virginia.

Veggie Lasagna

If you want to save time, use thawed, frozen mixed vegetables of your choice. Just make sure they are finely chopped.

▶ **DIFFICULTY: HARD**

Makes 4–6 servings

Play It Safe

Oven mitts or potholders are a necessity in every kitchen. Make sure you have both hands covered before touching any hot foods in the oven or on the stovetop.

1 egg
½ 15-ounce container (about 1 cup) part-skim ricotta cheese
1 cup shredded mozzarella cheese, divided
1 cup pasta sauce
6 no-bake lasagna noodles
1–1½ cups finely chopped vegetables, broccoli, onions, bell peppers, mushrooms

1. Preheat oven to 375°F. Spray a 9" × 9" square pan with cooking spray.
2. Beat the egg in a medium bowl. Add ricotta cheese and ½ cup mozzarella cheese. Mix well.
3. Spread ⅓ cup pasta sauce in bottom of prepared pan.
4. Top with 2 lasagna noodles. Spread ⅓ of the ricotta-mozzarella mixture on top of noodles. Sprinkle ⅓ of the chopped vegetables over top. Then, add another ⅓ cup pasta sauce.
5. Continue layering with 2 more lasagna noodles, another ⅓ of the ricotta-mozzarella mixture, another ⅓ of the vegetables, and the last ⅓ of the pasta sauce.
6. Finish layers with the last 2 lasagna noodles, the last ⅓ of the ricotta-mozzarella mixture, and the last ⅓ of the vegetables. Sprinkle remaining ½ cup of mozzarella cheese on top.
7. Cover pan with aluminum foil. Bake for 40–45 minutes, or until hot and bubbly.
8. Remove foil. Bake for an additional 5 minutes to brown the cheese on top. Let your lasagna cool for about 10–15 minutes before cutting and serving it.

Food Trivia

Cranberries, a traditional Thanksgiving food, were part of the Pilgrims' feast at the first Thanksgiving in 1621.

Fruity Rice

The apples and cranberries in this rice make it a nice autumn dish to go with a savory main dish like ham or Crispy, Crunchy Chicken Legs (Page 65).

▶ **DIFFICULTY:** HARD

Makes 4 servings

1 cup cooked rice
2 red apples
1 tablespoon oil
¼ cup raisins
¼ cup dried cranberries

1. Cook the rice according to package directions. Set aside.
2. Chop the apple into small pieces, leaving the skin on.
3. Heat the oil in a small skillet.
4. Add the apples and cook for about 5 minutes.
5. Stir in the raisins, dried cranberries, and rice.
6. Continue cooking and stirring until the rice mixture is heated throughout.

Bow Tie Pasta Primavera

If you don't have bow tie pasta, you can make this dish with any shape pasta you like. Broccoli, peppers, cherry tomatoes, zucchini, and yellow squash all taste yummy in this recipe, but you can use whatever fresh vegetables you have on hand.

▶ **DIFFICULTY: MEDIUM**

Makes 4 servings

1 12-ounce package bow tie pasta
1 tablespoon oil
3 cups chopped fresh vegetables
½ cup prepared pesto sauce
2 tablespoons grated Parmesan cheese

1. Prepare pasta according to package directions. Drain.
2. Heat oil in large skillet. Stir-fry vegetables until they are tender-crisp.
3. Add pesto sauce to skillet and mix. Add drained pasta. Stir to mix well. Top with Parmesan cheese to serve.

Jimmy likes . . .

. . . broccoli, but not bok choy

. . . cabbage, but not celery

. . . scallions, but not spinach

. . . zucchini, but not squash

. . . lettuce, but not lima beans

. . . peppers, but not parsley

Can you figure out the secret to which vegetables Jimmy likes?

Food Trivia

Like many other fruits and vegetables, peppers were first introduced to Europeans by Christopher Columbus.

Sweet Rainbow Coleslaw

Eating a "rainbow" of colorful foods allows you to enjoy a variety of good nutrition. All the different colors contribute different nutrients to your diet.

▶ **DIFFICULTY: MEDIUM**

Makes 4 servings

1 16-ounce package cut-up coleslaw mix with carrots
¼ cup chopped green pepper
¼ cup chopped red pepper
6 tablespoons vinegar
¼ cup sugar
3 tablespoons oil
2 tablespoons water

1. In a large bowl, combine coleslaw mix and chopped peppers.
2. In a small bowl, combine vinegar, sugar, oil, and water. Mix well.
3. Pour dressing over cole slaw and stir to mix well. Place in the refrigerator until ready to serve. Stir again before serving.
4. You can make this up to one day ahead of time.

Broccoli-Stuffed Baked Potato

Try stuffing your potato with other vegetables you like, too. Mushrooms, spinach, and bell peppers are all good choices.

▶ **DIFFICULTY:** MEDIUM

Makes 1 serving

1 potato
¼ cup fresh or frozen broccoli florets
¼ cup shredded cheese, any variety

1. Wash and scrub your potato under running water to clean it. Poke about 4 holes in the potato using a paring knife.
2. Cook the potato in the microwave for 5–6 minutes, until soft.
3. Cut the potato open wide. Set it aside for a minute.
4. Place the broccoli in a small bowl with about 1 teaspoon water and cook in the microwave for 1–2 minutes to soften and heat it. Remove from microwave and drain any excess water.
5. Stuff potato with broccoli and top with cheese. Place in microwave again and heat for 30 seconds to 1 minute, until cheese is melted.

Food Trivia

French-fried potatoes were first introduced in America when Thomas Jefferson had them served at a White House dinner.

WORDS to KNOW

paring knife: a knife with a small blade, used to cut small foods.

try This

Cut up 2 potatoes. Put one straight into a pot full of water. Leave the other out on the counter. What did you notice about the 2 potatoes? The one in the water didn't get brown, but the one on the counter did. Why? Because once you cut a potato, you expose its cells to the oxygen in the air, which causes the potato to brown. If you put the potato in water, the oxygen cannot reach the cells, so the potato doesn't brown.

Parmesan Potato Fries

You can prepare these potatoes with or without the skin in whatever shape you like. Before you know it, they'll be a favorite at your dinner table.

▶ **DIFFICULTY: HARD**

Makes 4 servings

4 potatoes
2 tablespoons oil
1 teaspoon salt
½ teaspoon pepper
1 tablespoon Parmesan cheese

1. Preheat the oven to 350°F. Spray a baking pan or cookie sheet with cooking spray. Wash the potatoes. Cut them into strips or rounds or any shape you choose.
2. Put the potatoes into a resealable bag or a large bowl. Add the oil to the bag or bowl and mix until the potatoes are well coated. Sprinkle the potatoes with salt, pepper, and Parmesan cheese. Toss again.
3. Place the potatoes in a single layer onto prepared baking pan or cookie sheet. Bake for 45–50 minutes, or until the potatoes are crispy and golden brown. Halfway through baking, flip the potatoes over so they cook evenly on all sides.

Chinese Fried Rice

Because this fried rice has eggs and vegetables, it is a good vegetarian meal all by itself. Fried rice is also a great way to use up leftover rice and vegetables.

▶ **DIFFICULTY:** HARD

Makes 4–6 servings

2 cups cooked white rice
¼ cup oil
1 small onion, chopped
2 cloves garlic, chopped
¼ teaspoon ground ginger

½ cup chopped carrots
1 zucchini, sliced
½ cup frozen peas
2 eggs, beaten
¼ cup soy sauce

Perfect Veggies

To see if the vegetables are cooked, stab one with a fork. If the fork goes in easily, your vegetables are done.

Tip

1. Cook the rice according to package directions. Set aside.
2. Heat oil in a large skillet.
3. Add the onion, garlic, ginger, carrots, zucchini, and peas.
4. Cook until the vegetables are tender, about 5 minutes.
5. Remove the skillet from the heat and put the vegetable mixture into a large bowl.
6. Add the beaten eggs to the skillet. Cook the eggs until they are scrambled.
7. Combine the egg mixture and the mixed vegetables.
8. Put the cooked rice into the skillet and stir.
9. Add the soy sauce to the rice, then add the vegetable and egg mixture back into the skillet.
10. Stir with the spatula until everything is heated through.

WORDS to KNOW

Dutch oven: a large, heavy pot with a tight-fitting domed cover good for making large quantities of soup, chili, and pasta

Vegetable Tortilla Soup

Make this as mild or as spicy as you wish, depending on what you and your guests or family like.

▶ **DIFFICULTY: HARD**

Makes 4 servings

1 teaspoon oil
1 onion, chopped
1 small tomato, chopped
¼ cup chopped green pepper
¼ cup chopped red pepper
1 teaspoon lime juice

4 cups vegetable or chicken broth
½ teaspoon salt
Dash pepper
Dash hot pepper sauce
1 ripe avocado, chopped
Tortilla chips

1. In a large saucepan or Dutch oven, heat the oil over medium heat.
2. Add the onion and cook for about 5 minutes, stirring frequently.
3. Add the tomato and peppers. Cook for about 2 minutes, until the vegetables are softened.
4. Add the lime juice, broth, salt, pepper, and hot pepper sauce.
5. Cook until fully heated throughout. Pour soup into individual bowls, and top with chopped avocados and tortilla chips.

Broccoli and Cheese-Stuffed Shells

You can use manicotti pasta instead of large shells. You will need to use a small spoon to stuff the cheese mixture inside the cooked manicotti.

▶ **DIFFICULTY: HARD**

Makes 6 servings

> ## Cooking with Cheese
>
> If the cheese begins to brown too quickly, cover the pan with a sheet of aluminum foil. This will keep the top from cooking too fast.
>
> *Tip*

6 ounces jumbo pasta shells

2 cups pasta or spaghetti sauce, divided into ½ cup and 1½ cup portions

1 egg, slightly beaten

1 15–16-ounce container ricotta cheese

2 cups chopped broccoli, fresh or frozen (thawed)

1 tablespoon parsley

¼ teaspoon salt

¼ teaspoon pepper

½ cup grated Parmesan cheese

1½ cups shredded mozzarella cheese, divided into 1 cup and ½ cup portions

1. Preheat the oven to 350°F.
2. Prepare the shells according to package directions. (Do not overcook the shells because they will be too soft to stuff. You can even slightly undercook them by 1–2 minutes.) Drain and cool.
3. Spread ½ cup of the pasta sauce into the bottom of a 9" × 13" baking pan.
4. In a large bowl, combine the beaten egg, ricotta cheese, broccoli, parsley, salt, pepper, Parmesan cheese, and 1 cup of the mozzarella cheese. Mix well.
5. Take a shell and stuff it with the cheese mixture, then lay the shell in the baking pan on top of the pasta sauce, cheese-side up. Repeat with the remaining shells.
6. Pour the remaining pasta sauce over the shells. Top with the remaining mozzarella cheese.
7. Bake for 25–30 minutes, or until the cheese is melted and lightly browned.

Creamy Corn Chowder

Try your chowder with a salad and fruit for a complete meal.

▶ **DIFFICULTY: HARD**

Makes 6 servings

1 tablespoon oil
1 onion, finely chopped
3 medium potatoes, peeled
   and chopped
2 cups water
½ teaspoon salt
¼ teaspoon pepper

2 tablespoons cornstarch
2 15¼-ounce cans corn,
   drained
2 cups milk
2 tablespoons butter or
   margarine

1. In a large saucepan, heat the oil over medium heat.
2. Add the onion and cook for about 5 minutes, stirring frequently.
3. Add the potatoes, water, salt, and pepper.
4. Turn up the heat and let sit until the mixture begins to boil.
5. When the soup starts to boil, reduce it to a simmer and continue to cook for about 20 minutes, or until the potatoes are tender.
6. In a separate bowl, mix the cornstarch with a little warm water to avoid clumps.
7. Add the corn, milk, and butter, and stir in the cornstarch to help thicken the soup.
8. Continue simmering for another 20 minutes, stirring occasionally. Cool slightly before serving.

FUN FACT

What is chowder?

Chowder usually contains seafood and vegetables (have you ever had New England clam chowder?)—but not always. Corn chowder is one of the exceptions. Chowder got its name from the French word for stew pot, the pot used to cook it.

Chapter 7

Desserts & Special Treats

1.

2.

3.

4.

5.

Cookies

In each of the cookies is the scrambled name of a fun food. Unscramble the words and write them in the proper spaces. Read the letters in the tinted spots from top to bottom to find the name of another fun food!

1. _ _ _ _ _ _

2. _ _ _ _ _ _ _

3. _ _ _ _ _ _ _

4. _ _ _ _ _ _

5. _ _ _ _ _

Sometimes, even when dinner has been delicious, you might have a **craving** for a certain sweet or dessert. That's when you can put your creativity to work and make something to satisfy your stomach. The desserts here are a lot of fun to make and can be shared with others as a special treat after a meal or in between. Make some for home or for special people like your grandparents, teachers, or friends. You will be so proud of yourself!

Double Chocolate Chip Cookies

Bake the cookies for 8 minutes for chewy cookies and longer (up to 10 minutes) for crispier ones.

▶ **DIFFICULTY:** MEDIUM

WORDS to KNOW

craving: a great desire, taste, or hunger for a certain food or beverage

Makes 2½ dozen cookies

½ cup sugar
½ cup brown sugar
½ cup butter or margarine, softened
2 eggs
½ teaspoon vanilla

1¾ cups flour
¼ cup unsweetened cocoa powder
1 teaspoon baking soda
¼ teaspoon salt
1 cup chocolate chips

1. Preheat the oven to 375°F.
2. In a large mixing bowl, use an electric mixer to combine sugar, brown sugar, margarine, eggs, and vanilla. Mix well until the batter is smooth.
3. Add the remaining ingredients, except for the chocolate chips.
4. When the batter is smooth and creamy, stir in the chocolate chips.
5. Drop dough by tablespoonfuls onto a cookie sheet.
6. Bake for 8–10 minutes, until golden.
7. Remove cookie sheet from the oven and let it cool 1 minute before removing the cookies.

Graham Ice Cream Sandwiches

Eat your ice cream sandwich right away or wrap it in plastic wrap and freeze it until you are ready to eat it.

▶ **DIFFICULTY: EASY**

Makes 2 ice cream sandwiches

4 graham cracker squares
½ cup ice cream, sherbet, or frozen yogurt of your choice, slightly softened
Candy sprinkles, optional

1. Place ¼ cup ice cream on one graham cracker square. Top with a second graham cracker square to make a "sandwich."
2. Dip the edges of the "sandwich" in candy sprinkles, mini chips, or nuts for an extra fun snack.

Cut the Cake

How would you cut a round cake into nine pieces with only four cuts of the knife?

Banana-Split Ice Cream Pie

What's better than ice cream after a cookout? Set out the fudge, whipped cream, cherries, and nuts so each person can top their own slice of pie.

▶ **DIFFICULTY:** MEDIUM

Makes 1 pie and about 8 servings

2 bananas
1 6-ounce ready-to-use graham cracker or chocolate piecrust
1 quart vanilla ice cream, softened
½ cup hot fudge sauce
Whipped cream
Maraschino cherries
Chopped nuts, optional

1. Slice bananas and lay them out in the bottom of the piecrust.
2. Scoop out the softened ice cream and spread it evenly over the bananas.
3. Freeze the pie for at least 2 hours to harden the ice cream.
4. Let the pie sit out for about 5 minutes prior to serving so it is easier to cut.

Food Trivia

People have been eating ice cream around the world for over 4,000 years, but only in the United States since the 1800s. In 1984, President Ronald Reagan named July National Ice Cream Month.

preserves: Fruit that is canned or made into jams or jellies for future use

Thumbprint Surprise

Try different flavors of fruit preserves to make these cookies more colorful.

▶ **DIFFICULTY: MEDIUM**

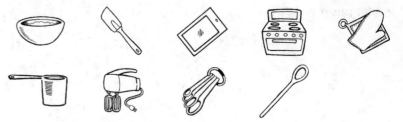

Makes about 4 dozen thumbprint surprises

1 cup (2 sticks) butter or
   margarine, softened
½ cup brown sugar
1 egg
1 teaspoon vanilla
3 cups flour

½ teaspoon salt
About ½ cup sugar, set aside
   on a small plate or saucer
½ cup jelly, jam, or preserves,
   any flavor

1. Preheat the oven to 350°F.
2. In a large mixing bowl, use an electric mixer to cream the butter and brown sugar until smooth.
3. Add the egg and vanilla and mix together.
4. Gradually mix in the flour and salt, stirring with a spoon as the batter becomes stiffer.
5. Scoop up about 1 tablespoon of dough and roll it into a ball, about 1" in size.
6. Roll the dough in the set-aside sugar to coat the outside of the ball.
7. Put the balls onto an ungreased cookie sheet, leaving about 2" between each cookie.
8. Slightly press down on the ball with your thumb to form a well in the middle.
9. Place about ½ teaspoon of jelly into each well.
10. Bake 10–12 minutes, until cookies are lightly browned.

Favorite Fudge

For a rocky road fudge, add chopped nuts or even mini marshmallows to the fudge before refrigerating.

▶ **DIFFICULTY:** MEDIUM

FUN FACT

The price of sugar

In 1900, sugar sold for $.04/pound. Today, it sells for more than 10 times that amount.

Makes 2 dozen pieces

3 cups sugar

1½ sticks butter or margarine

⅔ cup evaporated milk

1 12-ounce package chocolate chips

1 7½-ounce jar marshmallow cream

1 teaspoon vanilla

1. Spray a 9" × 13" pan with cooking spray.
2. In a large saucepan, combine sugar, butter, and milk.
3. Stirring constantly, heat the mixture until it boils (which takes about 5 minutes).
4. Turn off the heat and remove the pan from the burner.
5. Add the chocolate chips, stirring until they melt.
6. Add the remaining ingredients and stir until the mixture is well blended.
7. Pour the fudge mixture into the prepared pan.
8. Refrigerate until the fudge hardens (at least 4 hours) before cutting.

Is It Done Yet?

To test for doneness, insert a toothpick into the center of the brownies. If the toothpick comes out clean, the brownies are done. If there is batter on the toothpick, the brownies need to cook another 1–2 minutes. Then test again with a clean toothpick.

World's Best Brownies

You will receive lots of compliments for these brownies because everyone loves them. They make a wonderful treat to share with teachers, friends, relatives, and other special people in your life.

▶ **DIFFICULTY: HARD**

Makes 1½ dozen brownies

1 cup flour
1½ cups sugar
¾ cup unsweetened cocoa
½ cup brown sugar
½ teaspoon salt
½ cup (1 stick) butter or margarine, melted

3 eggs, lightly beaten
½ teaspoon vanilla
¼ cup semi-sweet chocolate chips
¼ cup white chocolate chips
½ cup chopped nuts, optional

1. Preheat the oven to 350°F. Spray a 9" square pan with cooking spray.
2. In a large bowl, use an electric mixer to combine the flour, sugar, cocoa, brown sugar, and salt.
3. Melt the butter in a small saucepan over low heat.
4. Add the melted butter, eggs, and vanilla to the sugar mixture. Mix well.
5. Fold in the semi-sweet and white chocolate chips, and nuts (if desired).
6. Pour the batter into the prepared pan.
7. Bake for 30–35 minutes, or until done.

Ultimate Peanut Butter-Chocolate Squares

You can't go wrong with these peanut butter and chocolate treats. Not only are they easy to make, they are a hit at every gathering.

▶ **DIFFICULTY: MEDIUM**

Makes about 3–4 dozen squares

¾ cup graham cracker crumbs
1 cup smooth peanut butter
1 cup (2 sticks) butter or margarine, melted
3½ cups confectioners' (powdered) sugar
1½ cups chocolate chips

1. Spray a 9" × 13" pan with cooking spray. Set aside.
2. In a large bowl, combine the graham cracker crumbs, peanut butter, melted butter, and confectioners' sugar. Mix well.
3. Spread batter out into prepared pan.
4. In a medium saucepan, heat 1 quart of water.
5. Put chocolate chips into a smaller saucepan and set this pan inside the saucepan of water to create your own double boiler. You can also use a specially designed double boiler if you have one.
6. Continue stirring chocolate chips until they are completely melted.
7. When the chocolate chips are melted, use a spatula to spread the chocolate over the peanut butter mixture.
8. Place pan in the refrigerator to cool before cutting into squares.

WORDS to KNOW

double boiler: made up of two saucepans, with one fitting inside the other

In this recipe, the larger saucepan heats the water. When the water boils, the chocolate in the smaller saucepan melts. This process allows the chocolate chips to melt slowly without being directly on top of the burner.

Food Trivia

Creamy peanut butter is preferred on the east coast of the
United States; chunky peanut
butter is preferred on the west
coast.

Chocolate-Peanut Butter Pudding

Try substituting chunky peanut butter for a crunchier taste.

▶ **DIFFICULTY: EASY**

Makes 4 servings

1 3.9-ounce package instant chocolate pudding
2 cups cold milk
½ cup peanut butter
¼ cup chopped nuts, optional
Whipped topping, optional

1. Prepare the pudding according to he package directions.
2. Use a whisk to stir the peanut butter into the pudding.
3. Pour the pudding into individual serving dishes.
4. Sprinkle with chopped nuts, if desired. Refrigerate until
   ready to serve. Add whipped topping, if desired.

Fruit and Cookie Pizza

When you place the fruit on the pizza, you can decorate it in any manner you want. You could spell out someone's name, make a flag for a holiday, or even create colorful patterns, like a rainbow.

▶ **DIFFICULTY: HARD**

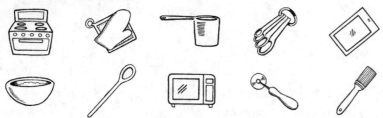

Makes 6–8 servings

1 16.5-ounce package refrigerated cookie dough

1 8-ounce package cream cheese, softened

¼ cup sugar

1 teaspoon vanilla extract

1 cup fresh fruit, cut up into slices/chunks (bananas, peaches, strawberries, blueberries, kiwi)

¼ cup fruit preserves, any flavor

2 teaspoons water

1. Preheat the oven to 350°F.
2. Spread entire roll of cookie dough out onto a large, ungreased pizza pan or cookie sheet. Bake 12–14 minutes, or until lightly browned. Remove from oven. Cool completely.
3. In a large bowl, combine softened cream cheese, sugar, and vanilla. Spread mixture over top of cooled dough.
4. Place fruit on top of cream cheese.
5. In small bowl, combine preserves and water. Heat in microwave for 30 seconds, until the glaze becomes liquidy and spreadable. Brush glaze over fruit on pizza.
6. Refrigerate your fruit pizza until you are ready to serve.

Mini Trifle

Try this with any variety of fruits you like. You could even add some chocolate syrup drizzled over the top for an extra-special treat.

▶ **DIFFICULTY: EASY**

Makes 1 serving

2 slices pound cake, cut into cubes
½ cup nondairy whipped topping
1 banana
4 strawberries, sliced
¼ cup blueberries

1. Start with a parfait glass, an 8-ounce tall, clear drinking glass, or a decorative glass bowl to build your trifle.
2. Layer pound cake, whipped topping, and fruit as you choose up and around the glass, reserving 1 tablespoon whipped topping and a strawberry slice for the top.
3. Top with the reserved whipped topping and strawberry slice.

Alternatives for knives

If you are concerned about using a sharp knife to cup your banana or strawberry, try using an egg slicer instead. It will easily cut through the soft fruit, and you'll get slices that are all the same size.

Fresh Fruit and Yogurt Parfait

Kids and adults alike will enjoy this fruit parfait. Try various types of fresh fruit and different flavors of yogurt to please everyone. Great for a quick, healthy breakfast, a snack or as a sweet ending to a meal.

▶ **DIFFICULTY:** EASY

Makes 1 serving

1 cup low-fat vanilla yogurt or vanilla frozen yogurt
¼ cup fresh raspberries
¼ cup fresh blueberries
¼ cup fresh blackberries
2 tablespoons granola

1. Start with a parfait glass. Spoon ¼ cup yogurt into bottom of the glass.
2. Add a layer of berries and top with more yogurt. Repeat the layers until all the ingredients are used up.
3. Top your parfait with the granola. Eat immediately.

You Scream, I Scream

Can you ever have too much ice cream? Maybe . . . see how you feel after you have eaten your way from START to END!

START

END

Chapter 8

Smoothies & Beverages

Drink Up!

Can you find the twelve beverages hiding in the glass?

FLOAT   **MILK**   **JUICE**
CIDER   **SODA**   **FIZZ**
SHAKE
PUNCH
ICED TEA
SMOOTHIE
HOT COCOA
LEMONADE

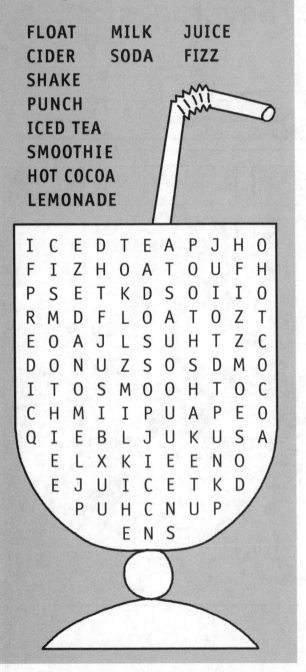

```
I C E D T E A P J H O
F I Z H O A T O U F H
P S E T K D S O I I O
R M D F L O A T O Z T
E O A J L S U H T Z C
D O N U Z S O S D M O
I T O S M O O H T O C
C H M I I P U A P E O
Q I E B L J U K U S A
  E L X K I E E N O
  E J U I C E T K D
    P U H C N U P
      E N S
```

If you have never made a smoothie or fun beverage at home, now is the time to try it. You will need a blender for some of these drinks, and most of them taste best in a nice, tall glass.

But those are the only rules! You can use fruit, yogurt, ice cream, milk, juice . . . anything that sounds like it might taste good. (And because they are mostly only one serving, if your concoction isn't so good, you haven't wasted too much in your experiment!)

Smoothies and floats are so easy to make and so delicious to taste. Once you've tried one as a breakfast drink or after-practice snack, they may just become your next favorite treat!

Creamy Shake

You'll go nuts over this creamy shake. You can freeze it for an extra-delightful treat.

▶ **DIFFICULTY: MEDIUM**

Makes 1 shake

1 cup frozen vanilla yogurt or ice cream
½ cup orange juice

1. Combine the frozen yogurt and the orange juice in a blender.
2. Put the lid on and blend for 1 minute, or until smooth.
3. Serve immediately in a tall, frosty glass.

Tropical Smoothie

For added decoration, garnish the glasses with a slice or two of fresh fruit. It's almost like you're on vacation!

▶ **DIFFICULTY: MEDIUM**

Makes 2 smoothies

1 cup orange juice
1 banana
½ cup frozen mango, papaya, or peach slices
½ cup frozen strawberries

1. Put all of the ingredients into a blender.
2. Put the lid on and blend for 1 minute, or until smooth. Pour into large glasses and enjoy.

Play It Safe

Tie back long hair and pull up long sleeves. First, you want to keep them out of your food. Second, for safety reasons you need to keep long or loose things away from things like blenders or the flame on your stove.

Keep electric appliances away from water or the sink. Also, try to keep the cords up on the counter so you don't trip or step on them by accident.

WORDS to KNOW

mango and ***papaya:***
tropical fruits with a sweet taste. Although they look different, they are both an orange-yellow color. Try each of them and enjoy.

Seeing Stars

All the vowels in this puzzle have been replaced. Oh my stars, can you still read the riddle?

WHY D*DN'T TH* *R*NG* CR*SS TH* R**D?

*T R*N **T *F J**C*!

Just Peachy Smoothie

This drink is best in the summer, when the freshest fruit is available.

▶ **DIFFICULTY: MEDIUM**

Makes 2 smoothies

2 cups vanilla frozen yogurt or ice cream
½ cup milk
1 medium fresh peach, peeled, pitted, and
    cut up into chunks (or ½ cup frozen peach
    slices, unsweetened)
1 tablespoon honey

1. Put all of the ingredients into a blender.
2. Put the lid on and blend for 1 minute, or until smooth. Pour into large glasses and enjoy.

Best Banana-Berry Smoothie

You can enjoy this smoothie any time of year. It's delicious, refreshing, and good for you. And it's a great choice for breakfast on the go!

▶ **DIFFICULT: MEDIUM**

Makes 2 smoothies

1 frozen banana
½ cup frozen berries, raspberries, blueberries, strawberries, or
any combination you choose
1 8-ounce container vanilla yogurt
½ cup milk

1. Put all of the ingredients into a blender.
2. Put the lid on and blend for 1 minute, or until smooth.
Pour into large glasses and enjoy.

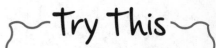

Try This

FREEZING A BANANA

When a banana becomes too ripe and soft to eat, you should freeze it to keep on hand for smoothies and frozen beverages. Peel the banana and then wrap it up in plastic wrap and place it in the freezer; otherwise, you will have a hard time removing the peel.

Grape Ice Delight

Use fun-colored straws and iced-tea spoons to get every last drop!

▶ **DIFFICULTY: EASY**

Makes 1 delight

2 scoops lemon or lime sherbet
½ cup grape juice
½ cup ginger ale

1. Put the sherbet into a tall glass.
2. Pour the grape juice over the sherbet and then pour the
ginger ale over the top.

FUN FACT

All about Grapes

Grape growing is the largest food industry in the world, with more than 60 species and 8,000 varieties. Grapes are eaten fresh, and they're also used to make juice and wine. The average person eats about eight pounds of grapes each year.

FUN FACT

Where did root beer first come from?

Many believe that root beer was first made by accident by a pharmacist trying to make a miracle drug by using roots, berries, and herbs.

Creamy Dreamy Root Beer Float

Watch the foam appear as you pour the root beer. What a treat!

▶ **DIFFICULTY: EASY**

Makes 1 float

2 scoops vanilla ice cream or frozen yogurt
1 cup root beer

1. Put the ice cream into a tall glass.
2. Pour the root beer over the top.

Food Trivia

Cola was first invented by mixing carbonated water into cough syrup.

There are 7,500 varieties of apples throughout the world.

Hot Apple Cider

Hot cider is a wonderful drink to serve at a party or to sip on a cool, fall night.

▶ **DIFFICULTY: HARD**

Makes 8 servings

8 cups (½ gallon) apple cider
1 orange, seeded and cut into thin slices
2 cinnamon sticks
6 cloves

1. In a large saucepan, combine the cider, orange wedges, cinnamon, and cloves.
2. Heat just to boiling.
3. Reduce the heat to a simmer and cook, uncovered, for 30 minutes. Remove the orange slices, cinnamon sticks, and cloves before serving.

Tangy Orange Fizz

Serve over ice. If you make a double batch for a party, pour the tangy orange fizz into a punch bowl with ice on the side so the punch doesn't get watery.

▶ **DIFFICULTY:** EASY

Makes 6 servings

2 cups lemonade
2 cups orange juice
2 cups sparkling water

1. In a large pitcher, combine all of the ingredients.
2. Stir well.

Try This

FLAVORED ICE

When you serve a beverage over ice, you can use flavored ice cubes if you like. Make a batch of lemonade or pink lemonade and pour the liquid into ice cube trays. When the ice is frozen, you can use it to flavor other beverages like punch, iced tea, or even Tangy Orange Fizz. Yummy!

Purple Cow

You will love this great taste combination. There's nothing better!

▶ **DIFFICULTY:** EASY

Makes 1 serving

¼ cup carbonated grape soft drink beverage
½ cup vanilla frozen yogurt or ice cream
½ teaspoon vanilla
2–3 ice cubes

1. Combine the grape soft drink, frozen yogurt, vanilla, and ice cubes in a blender.
2. Put the lid on and blend for 1 minute, or until smooth. Serve in a tall, frosty glass or mug.

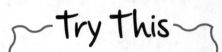

WORDS to KNOW

Carbonated
Carbonation occurs when carbon dioxide is dissolved in water, resulting in the "fizz." This fizz is also found in many soft drinks, which are carbonated.

I'm Thirsty

These kids are all thirsty, but everyone wants to drink something different. Crack the code on each glass to figure out who is sipping what. Remember—there's a different code on each glass!

1.
2.
3.
4.
5.
6.

Raspberry Smoothie

You could substitute strawberries or blueberries or use a combination here if you like.

▶ **DIFFICULTY: EASY**

Makes 1 smoothie

½ cup frozen raspberries
1 8-ounce container vanilla yogurt
¼ cup milk
1 teaspoon honey

1. Combine the raspberries, yogurt, milk, and honey in a blender.
2. Put the lid on and blend for 1 minute, or until smooth. Serve in a tall ice cream soda glass.

Food Trivia

Yogurt was first made thousands of years ago by nomadic tribes in West Asia and Eastern Europe. Today, Americans eat more than 300,000 tons of yogurt each year.

Chapter 9

Let's Play Some More

Kitchen creations are not all about food for meals and snacks. Making creative foods for holiday occasions and just for fun is a big part of cooking. There are so many recipes that you can make to serve at parties and for special occasions. Here are a few you may enjoy trying. Begin a collection of your own favorites, too.

You might also be surprised at what crafts you can make using common foods and ingredients. Bring out the supplies on a rainy day, during a slumber party, or even during an afternoon with the babysitter.

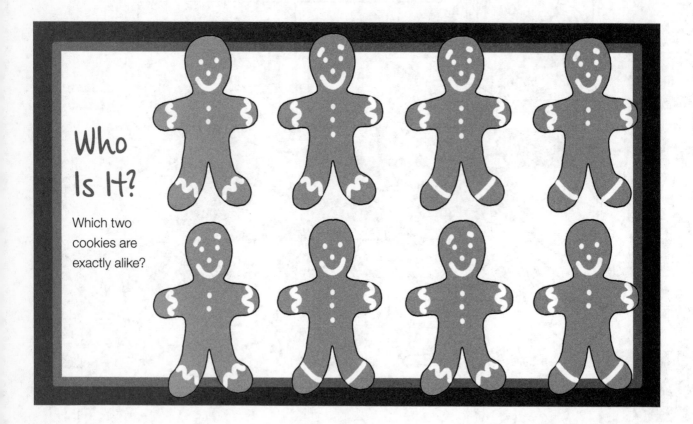

Who Is It?

Which two cookies are exactly alike?

Party-Time Punch

You can jazz up your punch by adding scoops of orange, lemon, or lime sherbet.

WORDS to KNOW

concentrate: a denser or stronger liquid that has water removed from it

▶ **DIFFICULTY: EASY**

Makes about 12 servings of punch

1 12-ounce can frozen orange juice concentrate, thawed
1 12-ounce can frozen lemonade concentrate, thawed
1 2-liter bottle ginger ale
2 oranges, seeded and cut into thin slices

1. Combine orange juice concentrate, lemonade concentrate, and ginger ale in a large punch bowl.
2. Mix well until the concentrates are dissolved.
3. Add orange slices to punch.
4. Add ice to keep cool, if desired.

Food Trivia

The average strawberry has about 200 seeds—they're those bumpy spots on the outside surface.

4th of July Cake

You will love decorating this cake for this special holiday. The entire family can help.

▶ **DIFFICULTY:** MEDIUM

Makes 12 servings

1 18.25-ounce yellow or white cake mix
1 16-ounce container prepared white frosting
1 pint fresh blueberries
1 quart fresh strawberries, sliced in half

1. Prepare cake mix according to package directions.
2. Once cake is completely cooled, spread with frosting.
3. Place 50 blueberries into upper-left corner, for the 50 stars on a flag.
4. Place strawberry halves in rows to signify the stripes on a flag.
5. Happy Independence Day!

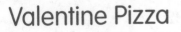

Valentine Pizza

You can decorate your pizza with any number of vegetables. The options are endless.

▶ **DIFFICULTY: MEDIUM**

Makes 6 servings

1 10-ounce package Italian pizza crust
¾ cup pasta sauce, any variety
1 8-ounce package shredded mozzarella cheese
Red, green, and yellow pepper slices
Fresh mushroom slices
Pepperoni slices

1. Preheat oven to 425°F.
2. Using kitchen shears, cut a wedge out of the round pizza crust to resemble a heart.
3. Spread pizza sauce over top of heart-shaped crust.
4. Decorate your heart using an assortment of cut-up vegetables or pepperoni slices.
5. Bake your pizza for 8–10 minutes, or until browned on top.

Food Trivia

On October 28, 2006, the Tiziano Shopping Centre in Italy set a world record for the longest line of pizzas ever displayed. The pizza line stretched for 186.3 meters. To give you some idea how long that is, go to the outdoor track at your local high school. See how long it takes you to run halfway around the track. That's 200 meters, a little bit longer than the pizza line in Italy.

~Try This~

**MAKE YOUR
OWN SPIDERS**

You can make your own gummy spiders from gum drops and thin licorice strings. Cut your licorice strings into eight small strips (legs) and insert them into the gum drop.

Halloween Spider Bites

You can use gummy spiders, gummy bats, gummy worms, or any other critters you choose on your webs.

▶ **DIFFICULTY: EASY**

Makes as many as you like

Flat chocolate wafer cookies
Small tube of white decorator gel
Toothpicks
Gummy spiders

1. Place chocolate wafer cookies on a cookie sheet or flat tray.
2. Using decorator gel, draw 3 circles on the cookie, one large one around the outside rim, a smaller one on the inside, and an even smaller one in the middle.
3. Using your toothpick, start at the inside middle of the cookie and run the toothpick all the way to the outside edge. Do this about 4 times around the cookie. This will create a "web."
4. Place gummy spider on top of your web.

Winter Wreaths

You can substitute colored sugars for the granola for a different twist.

▶ **DIFFICULTY: MEDIUM**

Makes 8 wreaths

1 8-ounce can refrigerated
   crescent rolls (8)
2 tablespoons milk, optional
1 drop green food coloring,
   optional

2 tablespoons sugar
½ teaspoon cinnamon
½ cup granola
8 maraschino cherries

1. Preheat the oven to 375°F.
2. Open the crescent rolls and separate them into 8 pieces.
   Use your hands to roll each crescent to a long skinny log,
   about 6"–8" long. Then connect the two ends to make a
   circle. These are your wreaths.
3. Put the milk in a small bowl, add in the food coloring, and
   mix. Using a clean pastry or paint brush, brush the green
   coloring on top of your wreaths. (You can skip this step
   and just make brown wreaths if you wish.)
4. Combine the sugar and cinnamon in a small bowl or
   shaker bottle. Sprinkle each wreath with cinnamon-sugar
   mixture. Sprinkle granola on top of the cinnamon-sugar
   mixture.
5. Bake 8–10 minutes, or until cooked and lightly browned
   around the edges.
6. Top each wreath with a cherry before serving.

try This

FOOD COLORING

Food coloring traditionally
comes in red, blue, green,
and yellow. Try mixing colors
to make new colors. Red and
yellow will make orange. Red
and blue make purple. Be
creative and try making your
own interesting colors.

FUN FACT All about cherries

There are more than 7,000 cherries on an average tart cherry
tree, depending on weather
conditions and the tree's age.
It takes about 250 cherries to
make a cherry pie.

Handmade Play Dough

Making play dough on a cold or rainy day can be just the project to keep you busy. It's also a fun way to spend time with your siblings and friends.

▶ **DIFFICULTY:** MEDIUM

Makes 2 cups of dough

2 cups flour
1 cup salt
4 teaspoons cream of tartar
1 package unsweetened powdered soft drink mix, any flavor or color, or several drops of food coloring
2 cups water
½ cup oil

1. In large saucepan, combine the flour, salt, cream of tartar, and powdered soft drink mix or food coloring.
2. Add the water and oil.
3. Heat on stovetop at medium heat and cook the mixture, stirring frequently.
4. As the mixture gets hot, it will turn into a thick dough.
5. When this happens, remove the pan from the stovetop.
6. Let the dough cool before you dump it out and play with it.

Store dough properly

This play dough may seem softer to you than the kind you buy at the store. It is so easy to squeeze and squish, but it might be a little more difficult to mold. If you store your dough properly in an airtight container or resealable plastic bag, it should last for a long time.

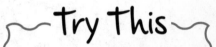
Making Bubbles

Making bubbles is always a blast. If you want to make different colored bubbles, just add a few drops of food coloring to your solution.

▶ **DIFFICULTY: EASY**

Makes about 1 quart of bubble solution

3 cups water
1 cup Joy brand dishwashing liquid (for some reason this is the
 brand that works best)
⅓ cup light corn syrup
Bubble wands, any size or shape

1. Mix the water, dishwashing soap, and corn syrup together
 in an airtight container with a tight cover.
2. Once the solution is mixed well, you can either use it
 straight out of the container or put the solution into a
 shallow bowl so more people can reach it at once.

try This

GET CREATIVE
If you don't have an old wand
left over from other jars of
bubbles, you can make your
own out of a wire hanger or
a plastic strawberry basket.
Experiment with different
sizes and shapes, and see
what happens!

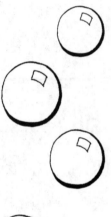

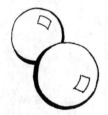

Cereal Necklaces

You can make these necklaces on regular string and take them in the car for an enjoyable snack. Or try making them at a party as an activity and a party favor.

▶ **DIFFICULTY: EASY**

Make as many as you like

1 cup O-shaped cereal (like Cheerios, Froot Loops, or any other brand)
Long, thin licorice strings

1. Put each different type of cereal into the separate cups of a muffin tin.
2. Hold onto the licorice string and thread on different Os in different patterns or colors—or flavors! (Make sure one end of the string is knotted; otherwise, your Os will come sliding right off!)
3. Knot the ends together to wear the necklace or just eat it as is.

The silly answer is, "It was a total flop!"

What's the silly question? To find out, use the rules to cross words out of the grid. Read the remaining words from left to right and top to bottom.

Cross out...
...fruits that are red
...three-letter words with E
...words that rhyme with FLOP

APPLE	DROP	HOW	EAT
CHOP	DID	POMEGRANATE	SHOP
BET	POP	CHERRY	YOUR
PINEAPPLE	HEN	CROP	STRAWBERRY
MOP	UPSIDE DOWN	TOE	CAKE
HOP	STOP	TURN	TOP
OUT	HEW	RASPBERRY	WET

Edible Finger Paints

This is an easy project for a rainy day. Not only will you enjoy creating it, but maybe your parents will take part in the fun, too. Use plain paper or coloring books to show off your creativity and enjoy your creations!

edible: able to be eaten

▶ **DIFFICULTY: EASY**

Makes about 2 cups of paint

1 3.9-ounce package instant vanilla pudding
2 cups cold water
Food coloring

1. In a large bowl, use a whisk to combine the pudding mix with the cold water.
2. Pour the mixture into a muffin tin or several small bowls.
3. Stir several drops of food coloring into each bowl to make different colors.
4. Refrigerate for 10–15 minutes before painting.

Play It Safe

Know where to find things and where to put them away. By keeping everything in its place, you will have a clean cooking area, and you won't lose things.

Even though this "paint" is **edible**, remember that lots of hands and fingers have been in it. After painting and playing with the paints, you probably want to limit the amount that goes into your mouth.

Graham Cracker Houses

Try making these during the holidays to create festive, decorated creations. Put your house on display or gobble it up!

▶ **DIFFICULTY: EASY**

One house of your very own design

4 or more graham cracker rectangles
½ cup peanut butter
Various tubes of decorating icing
Candy shapes like gumballs, gumdrops, chocolate chips,
    Hershey's Kisses, M & M candies
Cookie decorations like candy sprinkles, stars, and silver balls

1. Place a graham cracker on a flat surface.
2. Spread a thin layer of peanut butter along all four edges.
3. Stand another graham cracker upright on one edge of the first graham cracker, using the peanut butter as the "glue" to hold your house together. Repeat with other graham crackers, using more peanut butter as necessary, until you have a house.
4. Add decorating icing, candies, and sprinkles to complete your home. Placing the candies and sprinkles in a muffin tin will keep you organized and make them easier to access.

Snack Attack

If you are planning to snack on your house, do so within a day or two of making it, as the icing and candy will harden and begin to get stale.

Chocolate-Dipped Surprises

A fondue pot will keep the chocolate melted longer. If you have one, set it out with a platter of mixed fruit and cookies. Guests at your dessert buffet can dip their own favorite treats.

▶ **DIFFICULTY:** MEDIUM

½ cup of the melted chocolate will make enough for about 10–12 dipped items

Milk chocolate melt pellets (found typically in craft stores
for candy making)
Pretzel rods or rings, fortune cookies, strawberries, or any
other treat
Waxed paper
Candy sprinkles, any color or type, optional
Nuts, finely chopped, optional

1. In a plastic or glass bowl, heat about ½ cup of the candy melts in the microwave for about 1 minute. Stir chocolate to make it smooth.
2. Dip the item of choice into the chocolate.
3. Place dipped item onto a cookie sheet lined with wax paper. (Once you've filled the sheet, you can place it in the refrigerator to help the chocolate harden faster.)
4. Before the chocolate hardens, top with candy sprinkles or nuts.

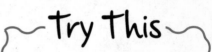

COLORED SURPRISES

Instead of using milk chocolate pellets, try white chocolate or even some of the other colors available, like red, for special occasions. These work just as well and can really jazz up your creations. A combination of different colors works great, too!

Candy Trivia

The candy bar Baby Ruth was named after the daughter of U.S. President Grover Cleveland in 1921. Tootsie Rolls were the first wrapped penny candy in America. The first bubble gum was introduced in 1906 and was called Blibber Blubber. Pez candies were first made as a breath mint.

In the Kitchen

Use everything you learned in this book to answer the questions below and fill in the puzzle grid on the facing page. Be careful—some of the answers are silly, not serious! We left you some T-I-D-B-I-T-S to help get you started.

ACROSS

1 After breakfast you eat _____.

3 All the recipes in this book taste _____!

5 A short name for a long sandwich

7 A crunchy shell filled with spicy meat and cheese

10 Do this to potatoes to make them fluffy.

11 It sounds like you have to "be a member" to eat this sandwich.

13 To cut a thin piece

14 Pot topper

15 You'll use one of these to flip a flapjack.

17 Important! Always do this before you start cooking!

21 Cut that carrot into tiny cubes

22 It would be great to have one of these to clean the kitchen!

26 Three-sided chips

30 Put something in a microwave and "____" it.

31 Yeast helps bread to _____.

32 Sweet and crunchy oats, seeds, and nuts that are good for breakfast or for snacks.

33 Why was the ice cream lonely? Because the banana _____!

DOWN

1 You can use this in a salad.

2 Tortilla chips with melted cheese on top

4 Baked 12 at a time in metal cups, they're sooo good, you'll eat them up!

6 Little, tiny vegetables are called "____."

8 Favorite round and chewy breakfast bread

9 Creamy soup that's good with corn or clams

11 A bowl with holes for water to drain out

12 What you find in the center of a cherry

16 The opposite of "rightunders"

17 You beat eggs and cream with this.

18 What does a gingerbread man put on his bed? Cookie _____!

19 These critters help bread to rise

20 On a hot day, it's good to drink cold lemon____.

23 A thin stream of liquid (or a light rain!)

24 This kind of Italian "pie" is a lunch and dinner favorite.

25 Use a spatula to _____ your flapjacks.

27 Waffle topper

28 Who likes "woofles" for breakfast? The ____!

29 A good thing to fill with ice cream

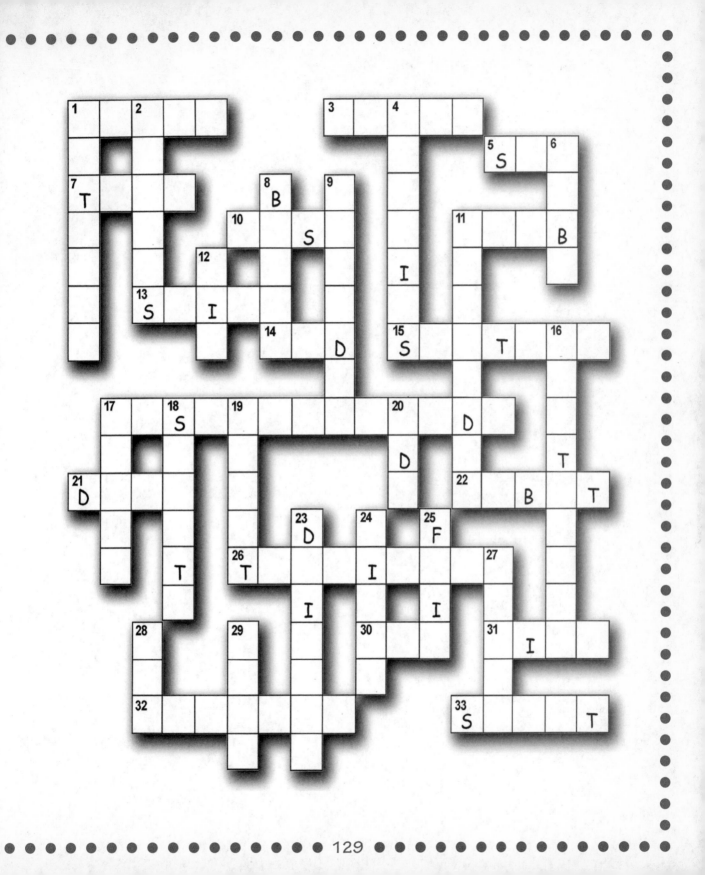

Appendix A
Online Resources

Once you spend some time in the kitchen, you may start looking for more recipe ideas. You may also want information on food or need a few tips on how to use some of your leftovers. The following Web sites are designed to be family friendly, so log on and see what you can discover as you continue to explore the kitchen!

www.kidshealth.com provides information on growing up healthy

MyPyramid.gov/kids is the USDA's site designed for kids from ages six to eleven. It includes games, worksheets, and detailed information about the new food pyramid.

www.idd-inc.com/pyramidtracker (directed toward seven- to ten-year-olds) helps kids learn about the Food Guide Pyramid and tracking their dietary intake.

www.zip4tweens.com teaches kids about incorporating beef in the diet through a variety of games and special features.

www.cdc.gov/powerfulbones offers good information on ways for girls to stay strong and take good care of their bones.

www.familyfoodzone.com shares information on growing and being healthy through nutrition, family fun, coloring, resources, and more.

www.pork4kids.com helps kids learn about eating pork through a variety of cartoons, games, recipes, and more.

www.whymilk.com by the creators of the "Got Milk" milk mustache campaign, teaches kids about the importance of drinking milk and including calcium and dairy foods in their diet.

family.go.com is part of Disney Online. It offers tips on healthful eating and snacking, food fun, recipes, and ideas for cooking with kids.

kidscook.com includes recipes, contests, and cooking kits.

kraftfoods.com/kf/yourkids shares cooking fun for busy families and kids.

wheatfoods.org shares information on the importance of wheat in the diet along with a collection of recipes.

www.foodchamps.org promotes a healthy diet of fruits and vegetables. A fruit- or veggie-shaped guide will show you the site's facts, games, and activities.

www.ars.usda.gov/is/kids focuses on science, farming, and agricultural activities and information for kids.

www.dole5aday.com helps kids learn the importance of eating five fruits and vegetables each day through a variety of games and fun activities.

Appendix B
Glossary

Alot of the terms in this book were explained in Chapter 1, but others are mixed in with the recipes. Here, all of your important terms are listed alphabetically. If you want to know about a word that's not in this list, look in the dictionary or ask an adult. Understanding cooking terms helps you know what you're doing in the kitchen. It also helps you know what you are getting the next time you eat out.

appetizer　a food or drink that stimulates the appetite and is usually served before a meal

bake　to cook something inside the oven

baking pan　a square or rectangular pan (glass or metal) used for baking and cooking food in the oven

basting　to moisten at intervals with a liquid (such as melted butter or pan drippings) during cooking

batter　a mixture made from ingredients like sugar, eggs, flour, and water that is used to make cakes, cookies, and pancakes

beat　to mix hard with a spoon, fork, whisk, or electric mixer

blend　to mix foods together until smooth

blender　an electric appliance used for blending liquids and grinding food

boil　to cook in a liquid until bubbles appear or until a liquid reaches its boiling point (water boils at 212°F/100°C). Note: Water cannot get hotter than its boiling point; it can only make steam faster.

bon appetit　French for "enjoy your meal"

broil　to put food under the broiler part of the oven, where the heat source is on top of the food

brown　to cook at low to medium heat until foods turn brown

buffet　a meal where many foods are set out on a table and people walk around and take what (and how much) they want

can opener　a tool, either manual or electric, designed to open cans

carbonation　occurs when carbon dioxide is dissolved in water, resulting in the fizz found in many soft drinks

casserole dish　a glass dish, usually a 1-quart or 2-quart size, used to make casseroles or baked mixtures in the oven

chill　to refrigerate food until it is cold

chop　to cut food into small pieces with a knife, blender, or food processor

colander　a metal (or sometimes plastic) pan or bowl with holes in it used to drain water or liquids from foods (such as pasta or vegetables)

concentrate　a denser or stronger liquid that has water removed from it

confectioners' sugar　finely powdered sugar with cornstarch added

cookie sheet　a flat metal sheet used for baking cookies or other nonrunny items

cool　to let the food sit at room temperature until it is no longer hot

craving a great desire or hunger

cream to mix ingredients like sugar, butter, and eggs together until they are smooth and creamy

cutting board a board made from wood or hard plastic used when cutting or chopping ingredients

dice to chop food into small, square (like dice), even-sized pieces

drain to pour off a liquid in which the food has been cooked or stored

drizzle to sprinkle drops of liquid, like chocolate syrup or an icing, lightly over the top of something, like cookies or a cake

Dutch oven a heavy pot with a tight-fitting domed cover

edible able to be eaten

electric mixer an electric appliance used for mixing ingredients (like cake batter) together

fold to gently combine ingredients together from top to bottom until they are just mixed together

garnish to add colorful and tasty "decorations" to a meal

glass measuring cup a glass cup with various measurements printed along the side, used to measure liquids

grate to shred food into tiny pieces with a shredder, blender, or food processor

grease to rub a baking pan or a dish with butter, margarine, or oil so food cooked on it won't stick

hummus a Middle Eastern dish that is a mixture of mashed chickpeas, garlic, and other ingredients, used especially as a dip for pita

ice cream scoop a plastic or metal tool, shaped like a giant spoon, used to scoop ice cream from a carton

kitchen shears kitchen scissors used for cutting foods

knead to fold, press, and turn dough to make it the right consistency

knives sharp utensils used for cutting, slicing, or carving (Always be careful when using knives—good ones are very sharp!)

measuring cups plastic or metal cups in different sizes, used to measure dry ingredients

measuring spoons plastic or metal spoons in different sizes, used to measure smaller amounts of both liquid and dry ingredients

microwave oven a small oven that cooks food very quickly by cooking with electromagnetic waves (microwaves)

mince to cut food into very small pieces

mix to stir two or more ingredients together until they are evenly combined

mixing bowls bowls in which you mix ingredients together

molasses the thick, brown syrup that is separated from raw sugar during the refining process

muffin tins metal or glass pans with small, round cups used for baking muffins and cupcakes

opaque cloudy; not clear or transparent

oven a kitchen appliance for baking or broiling food

oven mitts/potholders mittens or pads used to hold hot pots, pans, baking sheets, and plates

parfait glass   a special glass used to serve parfaits; it usually has a wide mouth and a narrower bottom

paring knife   a knife with a small blade, used to cut small foods

pastry brush   a small brush used to spread melted butter or margarine or sauces over food

pie plate   shallow dish made of glass or metal, used for making pies

pitted   without the center pit (as in peaches, olives, or avocados)

pizza cutter   a tool with a rolling cutter used to easily cut pizzas, dough, or breads

plate   a flat dish used to serve food

potato masher   a tool used to mash cooked potatoes—or anything soft—to make them smooth

preheat   to turn the oven on to the desired temperature and let it heat up before using it for cooking

preserves   fruit that is canned or made into jams or jellies for future use

puree   to mix in a blender or food processor until food is smooth and has the consistency of applesauce or a milkshake

resealable plastic bag   a bag with a zipper lock that can be easily closed to keep foods fresh

ripe   fully developed and ready to be eaten

rolling pin   a wooden or plastic roller used to flatten items such as dough for a piecrust

rubber spatula   a tool used for removing batter or liquids from the sides of a bowl

saucepan   a pot with a projecting handle used for stovetop cooking

sauté   to cook food on the stovetop in a skillet with a little liquid or oil

serving spoon   a large spoon used to scoop out large portions of food

simmer   to cook over low heat until the food almost boils

skillet   a pan used for frying, stir-frying, and sautéing food in hot fat or oil

slice   to cut food into even-sized slices

spatula   a flat metal or plastic utensil used to lift, turn, and flip foods like eggs, cookies, and hamburgers. A rubber spatula is helpful for getting foods out of jars, scraping batter, and spreading icings.

steam   to put food over a pan of boiling water so the steam can cook it

stir   to continuously mix food with a spoon

stir-fry   to cook food on the stovetop in a very hot pan while stirring constantly

stove   a kitchen appliance with gas or electric burners used for cooking food (also called a range)

tortilla   a round, flat, thin cornmeal or wheat-flour bread usually eaten with hot topping or filling

vegetable peeler   sometimes called a potato or carrot peeler, used to peel the skin off of fruit or vegetables

whip   to beat rapidly with a whisk, electric mixer, or an eggbeater

whisk   a utensil used for mixing and stirring liquid ingredients, like eggs and milk, together

wooden spoon   a big spoon made out of wood that is used for mixing and stirring just about any kind of food

Page 7 • Crazy Cookbooks

1000 PASTA DISHES, BY MACK A. RONEY
1 1 3 5 8 4 1 4 2 8

QUICK COOKING, BY MIKE ROE WAVE
5 3 4 4 3 8 3 2 4 2 7 1 6 2

YUMMY VEGETABLES, BY BROCK O'LEIGH
8 5 8 6 2 1 1 2 8 4 4 2 3

MEXICAN MEALS, BY AUNT CHILADA
2 3 1 2 1 8 1 3 1 1

LOSE WEIGHT!, BY CAL O. REEZE
4 2 7 2 3 8 1 4 2 2 2

Page 8 • Yummy!

A. Lettuce tossed with dressing
S A L A D
1 25 17 18 22

B. Melted rock from a volcano
L A V A
26 16 12 14

C. Sound that bounces back
E C H O
13 5 10 2

D. Back edge of the foot
H E E L
3 24 21 8

E. An adult boy
M A N
23 11 19

F. A baby bear
C U B
20 7 15

G. A female deer
D O E
9 6 4

Why did the circus lion eat the juggler?

SO HE COULD HAVE A BALANCED MEAL!

Page 10 • Measuring Spoon Math

Flour = __32__ Tbsp.

Sugar = __24__ Tbsp.

Cocoa = __4__ Tbsp.

Page 14 • A Tasty Puzzle

W A T E R
S H O R T E N I N G
O E
A hot potato!
N U T R I E N T S
E R U U
Y E What do you call a stolen yam? T G
L A B E L S A
T R

Page 16 • Breakfast Scrambles

1. What does a centipede have for breakfast?
   B A C O N AND L E G S

2. What does a lighthouse keeper have for breakfast?
   B E A C O N AND E G G S

3. What does a spook have for breakfast?
   G H O S T T O A S T

Bunches of Bagels

Page 19 **Bagel #1** is topped with PEANUTBUTTER.

Page 20 **Bagel #2** is topped with HUMMUS.

Page 25 **Bagel #3** is topped with GRAPE JELLY.

Page 28 **Bagel #4** is topped with CREAMCHEESE.

Page 29 **Bagel #5** is topped with EGG SALAD.

Page 22 • What's So Funny?

The secret to "Cooktalk" is to add the word "EGG" after every letter! When you remove all the extra EGGs, here is the riddle that remains:

What two things can't you have for breakfast? Lunch and dinner!

Page 32 • Silly Slice

ONE IS EASY TO CHEAT, AND THE OTHER IS CHEESY TO EAT!

Page 37 • Lunch?

A peanutbutter and jellyfish sandwich!

Page 40 • Mystery Meal

This recipe makes: Macaroni and Cheese

Page 44 • The Soup Pot

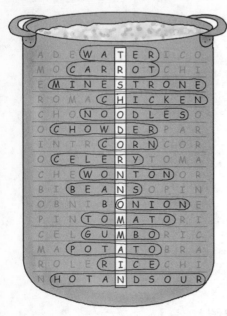

Page 54 • Sorting the Snacks

There are 8 different kinds of snacks.

popcorn   almond   wheat cracker   peanut

jellybean   pretzel   cheese puff   potato chip

There are 16 kernels of popcorn, and only 15 jellybeans. There is only one cheese puff!

Page 58 •
The Apple Barrel

The boys can cook up a delicious pot of applesauce, and spoon it out evenly into four bowls. Yum!

Page 62 •
Chef Andrew

1. Baked Beans
2. Cole Slaw
3. Rolls
4. Chicken Fingers
5. Iced Tea

Page 48 • Chips and Dip

Page 52 •
Leftovers

COLUMN A

CUP CAKE
STRAW BERRY
POTATO SALAD
PEANUT BUTTER
POP CORN
CORN CHIPS
COLE SLAW
HOT DOG
HAM BURGER
FRENCH FRIES
TUNA MELT
APPLE SAUCE
EGG ROLL

Page 72 •
Oodles of Noodles

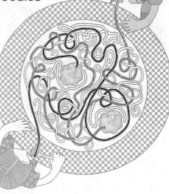

Page 76 • Kiss the Cook

RIBBIT!

Page 79 •
Hidden Veggies

1. Chop each carrot very carefully!
2. Abe answered "I love lettuce!"
3. Can you spin a cherry?
4. Fill the cab! Bag each vegetable!
5. The bee tasted the broccoli.

Page 81 • **Surprise Salad**

Page 106 • **You Scream, I Scream**

Page 85 •
Jimmy Likes . . .

Jimmy only likes vegetables that have double letters in them!

Page 108 • **Drink Up**

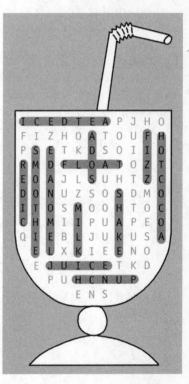

Page 94 • **Cookies**

1. W A F F L E

2. P U D D I N G

3. N O O D L E S

4. E G G R O L L

5. F R I E S

Page 96 •
Cut the Cake

Page 110 • Seeing Stars

WHY DIDN'T
THE ORANGE
CROSS THE
ROAD?

IT RAN OUT
OF JUICE!

Page 114 • I'm Thirsty

1. **MILK** *(Code is a simple number substitution, 1=A, 2=B, etc.)*
2. **SODA** *(Word is turned upside down and backward.)*
3. **SHAKE** *(Word is represented by a picture of a person shaking.)*
4. **WATER** *(H_2O is the chemical formula for water.)*
5. **JUICE** *(For each letter in the word, substitute the letter before it in the alphabet.)*
6. **ICED TEA** *(Word is represented by a picture of the letter "T" with icicles hanging on it.)*

Page 116 • Who Is It?

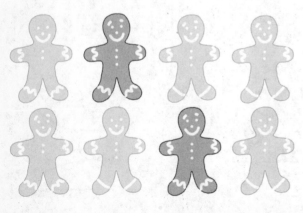

Page 124 • The silly answer is, "It was a total flop!"

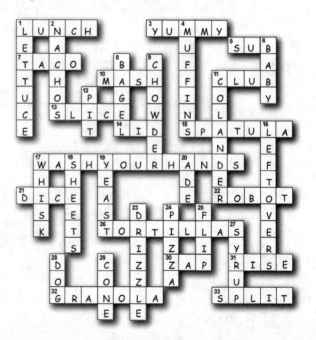

"How did your pineapple
upside down cake turn out?"

Page 129 • In the Kitchen

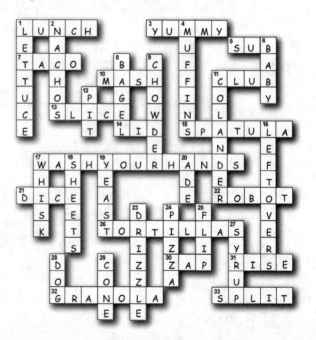